Concepts of Ideology

Concepts of Ideology

Howard Williams
Lecturer in Political Theory
University College of Wales, Aberystwyth

WHEATSHEAF BOOKS · SUSSEX
ST. MARTIN'S PRESS · NEW YORK

First published in Great Britain in 1988 by
WHEATSHEAF BOOKS LTD
A MEMBER OF THE HARVESTER PRESS PUBLISHING GROUP
Publisher: John Spiers
16 Ship Street, Brighton, Sussex
and in the USA by
ST. MARTIN'S PRESS, INC.
175 Fifth Avenue, New York, NY 10010

British Library Cataloguing in Publication Data

Williams, Howard Ll (Howard Lloyd), 1950–
    Concepts of ideology.
    1. Ideology
    I. Title
    145

    ISBN 0-7450-0380-X

Library of Congress Cataloging-in-Publication Data

Williams, Howard (Howard L.)
    Concepts of ideology and the ideology of fascism/Howard
Williams.
        p.   cm.
    'Wheatsheaf books.'
    Bibliography: p.
    Includes index.
    ISBN 0-312-01974-2: $30.00 (est.)
    1. Fascism.   2. Ideology.   I. Title.
JC481.W534 1988   87-37590
320.5'33—dc 19   CIP

Typeset in 11/12pt Times by
Just Words Phototypesetters, Ellen Street, Portslade, Sussex

Printed and bound in Great Britain by
Biddles Ltd, Guildford and King's Lynn

JEN

Contents

Preface

The object of this book is to provide as clear an introduction as possible to the notion of ideology. I intend to do so by looking at three contrasting views of ideology: the Marxist view; the view presented by the early political sociologist, Karl Mannheim; and the view presented by a neo-idealist group of English scholars, the Oakeshottians—followers of the political philosopher Michael Oakeshott. Clearly this does not represent an exhaustive list of the possible views of ideology nowadays available, but I aim to concentrate on these accounts since, taken together, they evince a certain symmetry.

The Marxist account is, no doubt, the most influential of the three. This is perhaps because of its continuing adaptability. It has many competing contemporary adherents. On the whole these adherents stand on the left politically. Mannheim's contribution to the development of the theory of ideology is a particularly prominent one. Writing for the most part in the 1920s and 30s, he offered a moderate, revised account of ideology which provided those nearer the political centre with an academically more conducive explanation for the beliefs held by individuals and groups. The third account of ideology I look at, the Oakeshottian, generally figures less prominently in the literature. I have, none the less, chosen to look at it not only because it provides an account of ideology which is agreeable to those on the right, but also because it appears to be founded on a number of common usages of the term. Looking at the Oakeshottian account provides us not only with a full sweep from left to right of views of ideology, but also draws to our attention certain common conceptions of the meaning of ideology which any satisfactory account of ideology must take into account.

The book is primarily intended for undergraduates taking courses in social, political and cultural studies who are looking for an introduction to a concept employed ever more frequently in their disciplines. I have assumed such students will want to know more about the origins of the concept they are being asked to use and something about the range of meanings it can convey. For this reason I also include in the book an important case study of Fascist ideology, where I attempt to demonstrate the illuminating way in which the three contrasting accounts of ideology can be brought to bear on a particular example of ideological thinking. The case study is valuable in that it provides an opportunity to evaluate the three theories of ideology and establish their usefulness (or otherwise) in explaining social and political events.

The term ideology has its origins in the philosophy of the French materialists of the eighteenth century. Drawing on the philosophy of the Englishman, John Locke, the French materialists developed a strongly anti-religious and pleasure-seeking view of the world. These were the philosophers of the Enlightenment. Such materialists as d'Alembert, Helvétius and Diderot played an important role in producing the climate of ideas from which the French Revolution was born. The first French materialist to employ the term ideology to describe their view of the world was Destutt de Tracy. In his *Elements of Ideology*, written between 1801 and 1815, Tracy used the term to describe that science of ideas which could be developed from the materialist perspective.[1] Following Locke, Tracy believed that all our ideas could be traced to their source in our senses.[2] For Tracy, thinking is a form of feeling. Words merely encapsulate what our sensations tell us. It follows that if we alter our sensations or, rather, the environment that gives rise to those sensations, then our thinking also will change, But for Tracy, as for the other Enlightenment philosophers, the attack has first to be made on the inherited, out-dated ideas which clog up our minds. One of the main objects of the science of ideas he proposed was to criticize our received cultural, social and religious conceptions and put in their place emancipatory ideas.

It is no coincidence that Tracy proposed his science of ideas or ideology at a time when public education was developing in France. His purpose was to provide the new secular educators with a systematic educational theory. The unashamed view of the ideologues, as followers of Tracy's philosophy were called, was that the minds of the young should be bent to new, more healthy purposes.

In the first instance, the teachings of Tracy and his ideologues met with the approval of Napoleon Bonaparte.[3] Napoleon even became an honorary member of the *Institut de France*, which was established in 1795 to propagate the ideas of the Enlightenment. However, subsequent to his rise to power and the eventual establishment of his empire, he began—in all too familiar a pattern with those who come to power as a result of a revolution—to find the critical ideas of his former philosophical mentors very troublesome. Having made his own peace with the Church in the course of his rise to power, he found the critical, anti-religious attitudes of the ideologues an embarrassment to him. Consequently Napoleon began to refer contemptuously to the members of Tracy's school as *mere ideologists* who had little knowledge of the practical world. Thus a negative concept of ideology as impractical and doctrinaire became current and popular. It is this negative concept that is still widely held today.

Nowadays the use of the concept of ideology arouses in us a sense of suspicion about the set of beliefs—and the people who hold those beliefs—to which it refers. The generally current use of the term implies that there is something out of place with a person who defends an ideological standpoint. Historians of ideas have shown that the concept has never entirely been without this kind of connotation. It is usually assumed that the difficulty with ideological thinking is that it is too dogmatic where flexibility is called for, and that it is too self-assured where modesty and impreciseness are more appropriate.

The present suspicion of ideology has been intensified by the cold war of the 1950s and 60s and the subsequent rivalry between the superpowers. The leaders and citizens of the United States of America and the leaders and citizens of the

Soviet Union regard each other's governing social and political doctrines as ideological. Behind the Russian accusation of ideological bias in the western approach lies a detailed theory of ideology (which we shall discuss in the first chapter); behind the West's condemnation of the Russian approach as ideological lies a long history of intellectual tolerance and the acceptance of diversity in social and political beliefs.

The intriguing point about both these views of ideology is that each holds its opponent's view to be distorted or exaggerated in one respect or another. The views of the rival superpowers cannot be taken at face value since they reflect a complex ideology which may have its own hidden meanings and consequences. It is this sense of the term ideology which is most current in contemporary political science. No western academic's account of the Soviet political system is complete without a chapter dealing with ideology and no account of the history of a political party, both East and West, is similarly complete without reference to the party's system of ideas or ideology. Thus, political scientists have come to see ideology as an integral part of what is often called a society's political culture.

To facilitate the reader's task I have tried to distinguish as far as possible between the descriptions I give of the three views of ideology and the criticisms which I have to make of them. Each chapter opens, therefore, with as clear an account as possible of the view of ideology being considered and concludes with a separate section summing up my criticisms. The purpose of the criticisms is to induce in the reader a thoughtful and evaluative approach to the competing claims of the three theories of ideology. Issues of interpretation necessarily enter into the comprehension of social and political ideas, and one of the objects of this study of ideology is to make the student aware of this.

The study ends with a brief discussion of two of the more currently fashionable uses of the concept of ideology. Quite appropriately, these concepts are given to us by two modern French structuralist philosophers, Althusser and Ricoeur. In the conclusion I show that, despite the bewildering variety of uses to which the concept is put, the theory of ideology has an important role to play in understanding contemporary society.

NOTES

1. Cf. D. McLellan, *Ideology*, Open University Press, Milton Keynes, pp.5–6.
2. Cf. J. Larrain, *The Concept of Ideology*, Hutchinson, London, p.27.
3. Cf. *ibid.* p.28.

1 Marx's Account of Ideology

There are four main aspects to Marx's theory of ideology. The first aspect is concerned with the manner in which the economic basis of society conditions the thinking of the members of that society. The second concerns the effect the development of the division of labour has on our thinking. The third aspect concerns what Marx takes to be the chief weakness of ideological thinking: the way in which, in an ideology, the effects of history on our contemporary thinking and position are overlooked. The fourth aspect concerns the way in which ideological control manifests itself in the cultural dominance of the ruling class in society. Thus, the first deals with the relationship between what Marxists call the ideological super-structure of society and its economic basis; the second with various forms of the division of labour; the third with history; and the fourth with the ruling system of ideas.

DETERMINATION OF THE SUPERSTRUCTURE BY THE BASE

The main thesis of Marx's theory of ideology is that material production provides the foundation of human experience and is therefore of crucial importance in the formation of an individual's thinking. By the term 'material production' Marx and Engels mean what we would broadly call the economic sphere. Their view is that the economic sphere is the most important sphere of human existence, and colours all else, including our thought. This is a point that is stressed over and over again in the only work in which Marx and Engels deal at length with ideology, *German Ideology*, written in 1845–6 in Brussels, where they sought refuge from the German and French secret police.

'Consciousness', Marx and Engels say, 'does not determine life, but life determines consciousness.' So they suggest the premises from which they 'start are not arbitrary; they are not dogmas but rather actual premises from which abstraction can be made only in imagination. They are the real individuals, their actions, and their political conditions of life, those which they find existing as well as those which they produce through their actions.'[1]

Marx and Engels argue that there is every justification for taking production as primary in men's experience because production is an objective and real distinguishing feature of man:

Man can be distinguished from the animal by consciousness, religion, or anything else you please. He begins to distinguish himself from the animal the moment be begins to *produce* his *means of subsistence*, a step required by his physical organization. By producing food, man indirectly produces his material life itself.[2]

For Marx and Engels production is not a narrow, purely economic (as opposed to a social or cultural) function of man. They see the activity as wider than economic activity in the merely financial sense, and also as wider than economic activity in the merely manual, directly productive sense. Marx has in mind 'the totality of these relations of production'.[3] The relations of production are, for Marx, the sum of those relations of human individuals with nature which enable human beings to persist as a species. But 'this mode of production must not be viewed simply as reproduction of the phsyical existence of individuals. Rather it is a definite *mode of life*.'[4] The totality of our economic relations does not only enable our continued survival as individuals and as a society but also creates the overall context of our existence. In our economic activity, according to Marx, we express our life, and in expressing our lives we mould and create our character.

'The nature of individuals thus depends on the material conditions which determine their production.'[5] This is, as we can see, a far-reaching thesis which implies that not only our ideas but also our whole personalities are governed by what we do. In brief, Marx and Engels suggest that individuals *are* what they do: 'The ideas which these individuals form are ideas either about their relation to nature, their mutual relationship, or their own nature'.[6] We cannot form ideas of anything which lies outside our experience. So if the ideas of individuals are necessarily ideas about their experience: 'it is evident . . . these ideas are the conscious expression—real or illusory—of their actual relationships and activities of their production and their commerce, and of their social and political behaviour.'[7] But not only do we form our ideas in the context of the day-to-day production of our existence, the formation of ideas is itself a process of production. Thinking cannot be torn away from people's practical life experience because not only does this provide the context of their thought, but thinking itself is an integral part of the production of life. Thinking originates in the production process itself. It evolves at the same time as other human capacities from the struggle to wrest the means of existence from nature.

Marx and Engels sum this up by saying:

The production of ideas, of conceptions, of consciousness is directly interwoven with the material activity and the material relationship of men; it is the language of actual life. Conceiving, thinking, and the intellectual relationships of men appear here as the direct result of their mutual behaviour. . . . Men are the producers of their conceptions, ideas etc., but these are real, active men, as they are conditioned by a definite development of their productive forces and of the relationships corresponding to these up to their highest forms.[8]

All our thinking is related to and is connected with actual problems of our material social existence. True, thought is the product of the mind, but the mind should not be seen as a kind of disembodied soul which is not related to the external conditions of life. Marx and Engels would not accept the view of the Stoic philosophers of the third and second centuries BC: that we can abstract from the difficulties and problems of our day-to-day experience. The mind is always the mind of a distinct individual—an actual empirical person—who finds himself or herself, and his or her society as well, existing under distinct material circumstances. The empirical person thinks about these circumstances, he thinks about his relation to other individuals in the society, and may even think about his manner of thinking, but this thought is always conditioned by those material, actual social circumstances. Thus our economic circumstances, so to speak, set the stage for our intellectual activity and its expression.

Therefore, since 'consciousness can never be anything else except conscious existence, and the existence of men is their actual life-process',[9] where, according to Marx's critical criteria, our thinking does not properly reflect our circumstances and is therefore confused, this must be a product of those circumstances themselves. Here, of course, when Marx and Engels speak of confused ideas they do not have in mind the thinking of deliberate liars and madmen. What they have in mind are confused accounts of human existence, social life and the world, which are believed and accepted by sections and, even, the whole of society. This is ideological thinking. This is thought which does not explain and understand the true relationship of human individuals to each other and human individuals to the world, but is still commonly accepted as a satisfactory account of these relations. For instance, most Germans would nowadays accept that the racist ideology propounded by the Nazis in the 1930s was patently false, but this patent falsity did not prevent it from exercising a dominant hold over that society. Ideological thought is, in other words, all thinking which does not properly recognize the material basis of human existence and does not relate that to its own formulation.

One obvious example for Marx and Engels is religious thought. They argue that religious thought provides an explanation of human society and its origins, which, from a rationalist and scientific viewpoint, is clearly false. But the hold of religion can be explained, they believe, not from the cogency of its claim but from the nature of productive material and social relations in the contemporary world. Religion depicts man as an unworthy, alienated being. This alienation can be explained from the nature of society. An ideology such as the Christian religion does not appear from nowhere. Indeed, 'if men and their circumstances appear upside-down in all ideology as in a *camera obscura*, this phenomenon is caused by their historical life-process, just as the inversion of objects on the retina is caused by their immediate physical life'.[10]

Ideology for Marx and Engels comes into existence very much like any other natural phenomenon. It occurs because our material, productive lives are organized in such a way that it necessarily gives rise to confusions about our mutual relations. If there are 'phantom forms in the human brain' they are the 'necessary sublimations of man's material life-process'.[11] In outlining this view of ideology and knowledge, Marx and Engels' principal target is, as Parekh points out, 'the traditional view of rationality' where 'thinking was essentially a contemplative activity in which the human mind soared above the contingencies of human existence and comprehended its subject-matter without being influenced by any extra-rational factors issuing from the thinker's psychological or social background. Thinking, in other words, was regarded as a direct and unmediated encounter between the thinking mind and the objects of thought'.[12] This strikes not only at religious doctrines, which argue for the existence of an eternal human soul, but also at philosophical doctrines, which hold that all reality is ultimately thought. The ancient Greek philosopher Aristotle believed the highest form of human life was the contemplative life, free from the practical concerns of everyday human life. Marx and Engels see this as an illusion. Even the thinking of Aristotle, freed as he was from day-to-day labour by his slave, none the less reflected his material, practical concerns as a philosopher and member of his class.

Marx and Engels do not accept that thinking can be abstracted or cut off from all external factors. The social, cultural and economic background of a thinker conditions what the thinker concludes. Thus, if the individual draws false conclusions these may be understood, if not excused, from an intellectual point of view as necessarily arising from the individual's particular social standpoint. For Marx, ideologists are persons who do not fully recognize or acknowledge the influence of their particular social, economic position on the formation of their ideas. They are persons who mistakenly believe their ideas are shaped wholly independently of their circumstances.

THE DIVISION OF LABOUR

In the Marxian view, the development of the division of labour is more than anything else responsible for the emergence or growth of ideological thinking. If it were not too much out of tune with the secular spirit of Marx and Engels' doctrines we might describe the division of labour as the 'original sin' which gave rise to the 'innate' evil of ideology in human life. For the first form of ideologists are the witch-doctors and priests of primitive societies, who appear once there is sufficient economic surplus to sustain a member of the tribe without his being directly employed in production. The existence of such a priesthood (or some similar institution) and the growth of ideology are synonymous for Marx and Engels.

Indeed, 'the division of labour is a true division only from the moment a division of material and mental labour appears. From this moment on consciousness can really boast of being something other than consciousness of existing practice, of really representing something without representing something real. From this moment on consciousness can emancipate itself from the world and proceed to the formation of "pure" theory, theology, philosophy, ethics, etc.'[13]

The division of labour is a 'structural' cause of ideological thinking. In the first place, it makes thinking the separate activity of one group, abstracting this group from the rest of society. Thinking for the first time becomes a 'higher activity', hence the mysterious select quality of members of the priesthood. In modern society the complex division of labour is brought about by the development of the capitalist productive process. The modern factory and office contains within it the most advanced division of labour, relating to the tools and machinery used. Under the one roof one can have gathered the most vastly different skills, from electrician to seamstress. The division of labour within enterprises is most ramified also; one factory may be responsible for producing essential components for the other, just as the other may be producing indispensable raw materials for another factory or production sequence. This capitalist process of development goes on, Marx believes, for the most part behind the backs of the individual producers and very often against their own interests. Indeed, Marx shows in *Capital* how the further development of the division of labour in a manufacturing concern can lead to the individual labourer being thrown out of work. Technical innovation often leads to a requirement for fewer labourers.

For Marx and Engels 'the division of labour offers us the first example of the fact that man's own act becomes an alien power opposed to him and enslaving him instead of being controlled by him . . .'.[14] The modern capitalist division of labour, for instance, limits the development of the individual to one aspect of production. The individual is a journalist rather than a printer, a musician rather than a painter, assembles cars rather than designs them. This splitting up of roles and tasks under a capitalist employer leads to the productive process becoming the master of the individual, rather than the individual being the master of the production process. So there is a latent conflict between the interests of the individual and the interests of the society as a whole. Individuals come to view society as a dominating force above them. They are alienated. Individuals move their jobs, lose their jobs or find their wages fluctuating according to market forces which are wholly out of their control.

Marx and Engels argue that, until the present, the division of labour has determined the overall direction of production and not production the division of labour: instead of the producers themselves controlling production, the course of production controls the producers. As Marx says in *Capital*, 'the division of labour is a system of production which has grown up spontaneously and continues to grow behind the backs of the producers'.[15]

Thus he thinks it is only natural that the conceptions men create in conformity with these relations bear witness themselves to this confusion, and, indeed, foster it. In Marx's view ideology forms a 'vicious circle' which can only be broken at the level of economic activity. 'Bad' ideological ideas cannot on their own successfully drive out 'good' ideological ideas. The only lasting solution is to get rid of ideology altogether by ending the present, apparently naturally determined, division of labour. Marx imagines that 'in a Communist society, where nobody has an exclusive area of activity and each can train himself in any branch he wishes, society regulates the general production, making it possible for me to do one thing today and another tomorrow, to hunt in the morning, fish in the afternoon, breed cattle in the evening, criticize after dinner, just as I like, without ever becoming a hunter, a fisherman, a herdsman or a critic'.[16] In a Communist society the various types of productive activity will be regulated by the workers themselves so that the social relations which flow from this activity are perfectly transparent to those who participate in them. Where our social relationships are entirely clear to one another, then the confusion of ideological thinking vanishes.

This is a point that is better put by Marx in his major work *Capital*. There is an element of naïvety about the account of the ending of the division of labour in the early book, *German Ideology*. The notion that we can have a society where each individual is skilled in a vast variety of tasks is an unrealistic one. No one can effectively be 'a hunter, a fisherman, a herdsman and a critic', especially in the course of one day! The essence of Marx's later version of a Communist society is not that everyone can do what they like, but that the combined activity of producers should be regulated by a common plan. It is this common plan of production which brings the division of labour properly under society's control that ultimately dispels the confusions of ideology. As Marx puts it in *Capital*: 'The life-process of society, which is based on the process of material production, does not strip off its mystical veil until it is treated as production by freely associated men, and is consciously regulated by them in accordance with a settled plan'.[17]

IDEOLOGY AND HISTORY

Consciousness or thinking is for Marx and Engels a historical phenomenon. It is the product of the work and social activity of innumerable generations of people. At each stage in our development, they say, 'there is to be found a material result, a sum of productive force, a historically created relationship to nature and of individuals to each other which is inherited by each succeeding generation from its predecessors, a mass of productive forces, capitals and circumstances which is indeed on the one hand modified by the new generation but, on the other, also prescribes its own life conditions and gives it a specific development, a particular character . . .'.[18] What lies behind the historical phenomenon of consciousness is the conscious activity of generations of other human beings. Marx and Engels see consciousness, as Hegel does in the *Phenomenology of Spirit* as the product of the dialectical development of previous modes of thinking and forms of life.

Georg Wilhelm Friedrich Hegel (1770-1831) had an extraordinary influence upon the development of Marx and Engel's thinking. Both, at one time, regarded themselves as pupils of the great idealist philosopher and rose to prominence through their membership of a radical Young Hegelian group. Marx and Engels broke with this group in 1844, and their early work on *German Ideology* had as one of its main objectives the distancing of their thinking from that of their former peer group. Hegel was a far greater philosopher than any of his radical pupils Marx and Engels were attacking. Many of his ideas formed a model and a backcloth for the critical development of Marx and Engels's ideas. In the *Phenomenology of Spirit*, completed in Jena in 1807, Hegel sought to demonstrate how our thinking gradually emerges from simpler forms of consciousness, such as sense-awareness and perception. Hegel charts a gradual upward path from these forms to reason and, what he ambitiously calls, 'absolute knowledge'. Marx and Engels reject the notion that we can ascend to absolute knowledge but they accept the proposition (and incorporate it in their theory of ideology) that our consciousness is formed over time.

For Marx and Engels, ideological thinkers are those thinkers who fail to see the connection between their thinking and their historically determined circumstances. We are all limited, finite creatures living our lives under particular, limited circumstances. (Such ideological thinkers regard their ideas as entirely fresh and without previous history.) Marx attempts to give an explanation of how this happens in *Capital*, where he says:

Man's reflections of the forms of social life take a course directly opposite to that of their actual historical development. He begins, *post festum*, with the results of the process of development ready to hand before him. . . . The characters [which give things their identity] have already acquired the stability of natural, self understood forms of social life, before man seeks to decipher not their historical character, for in his eyes they are immutable, but their meaning.[19]

In one respect, therefore, history deceives us all. Since we, as well as the material and social phenomena we observe, are products of history we come initially to look at things in a way which is impregnated with the past. Our finest efforts to understand something cannot help but be influenced by previous conceptions and misconceptions. Let us, for example, take the idea of the nation. Looked at 'objectively', in Marx's view, the nation is an entirely artificial community. Most so-called nations do not even possess a common language, and even where this exists the presence of distinct and opposing classes within the nation prevents the growth of social harmony. But this is the nation viewed in a dispassionate, detached way. This is not how the nation first appears to us. We are all born members of one nation or another. The customs and practices of centuries have led us to see each other as belonging to one national group despite these conflicts. Young children in growing up learn to identify with the nation to which they belong. So although the nation, viewed dispassionately, is not a true community it is, nevertheless, perceived in this way. Moreover, the principal institutions of the society have grown up within the context of the nation-state. Power is held centrally in the capital of the state; the institutions situated in the capital foster a sense of national identity. So if we see our country 'upside-down' as a nation, it is because the country's institutions are, in a sense, 'upside-down' as well. It is the centralization which brings about (sometimes forcibly) the one culture and not the one culture which brings about centralization.

Those who write history for the most part belong to the society which is being studied. Moreover, they not infrequently belong to the ruling groups in that society. This is one reason which leads Marx and Engels to argue that history has until now been written 'according to an extraneous stan-

dard'.[20] The tendency of historians has been to detect intellectual trends in an epoch and to attribute underlying changes
to those trends. But Marx and Engels see such trends as
symptoms rather than causes. The acceptance of such supposed trends leads to what they call 'the illusion of an epoch',
namely the notion that there is a dominating intellectual trend
in an epoch which decisively affects the development of
society (an example might be the phenomenon of 'mone-
tarism' in the western economies in the 1970s and 80s). Often
what historians have tended to do is to share this 'illusion of
the epoch', attributing to it the power to shape events. Their
task should in fact be to unmask such illusions, instead of
being (more often than not) their victims. For example,
'When the crude form of the division of labour which is to be
found among the Indians and Egyptians calls forth the caste-
system in their state and religion, the historian believes the
caste-system is the power which has produced the crude social
form.'[21] Where even professional historians often see things in
an inverted form there is little wonder that the layman is led to
do the same.

In view of this, Marx and Engels argue, ideological thinking
will cease to have a hold only where those social, material
circumstances giving rise to it are removed. But there are
severe obstacles to removing the social circumstances which
give rise to ideology. This is because the ideology of an epoch
is the ideology of the ruling class of that epoch and so per-
meates the thinking of all social classes.

THE RULING CLASS AND IDEOLOGY

Ideologies for Marx are systems of misleading ideas about the
nature of man and society. They are, if one wishes, partial
accounts of life. These false accounts are the unavoidable
result of man's historical development and social and economic circumstances.

Of course, for Marx and Engels, 'the history of all hitherto
existing society is the history of class struggle'.[22] Beginning
with class society right through to modern capitalist society,
all communities have been divided into a controlling group

and a subservient group. The instrument of this control is, Marx believes, the domination of the means of production. Whoever controls the means of production controls the society as a whole.

So the dominant class at any one time is the dominant power in production. Since all ideas have their origin and context in the economic basis of society it follows for Marx and Engels that economic dominance at any point of time must be reflected in intellectual dominance. In other words, 'the ideas of the ruling class are in each epoch the ruling ideas'.

This is so because: The class which has the means of material production at its disposal, with that disposes at the same time over the means of intellectual production. Thereby, the ideas of those who do not have the means of intellectual production are on average subordinate to it. . . . Those ruling ideas are nothing more than the ideal expression of the ruling material relations, the ruling material relations conceived as ideal; therefore just the relations which make one class into the ruling class are the ideas of their dominance.[23]

People think as they live, and if a person is a member of a ruling class he or she should think as one such member. It is only natural that individuals should encourage the spread of ideas which are favourable to their class. And, with the increase and growth in the division of labour, the ruling class will employ a special group of intellectual producers to carry out this task for them. These people, according to Marx, 'make it the chief branch of their livelihood the development of the illusions of this class about itself'.[24] These are ideologists in the most vulgar and pejorative sense of the term.

The sub-title of Marx's major work *Capital* is 'a critique of political economy'. Marx's object in the work is to build up a clear account of the shortcomings of capitalism based upon the work of previous investigators. Marx regards most of these investigators (apart from the few socialist critics of capitalism) as bourgeois ideologists. However, he distinguishes carefully between those classical political economists who take an objective approach to their discipline and the later vulgar political economists who neglect the scientific aspects of the discipline and become mere apologists for the status quo. Marx takes Adam Smith, Ricardo and John Stuart

Mill to be the major classical economists; in the category of vulgar economists he places individuals such as Nassau Senior, who made a name for himself as a defender of the twelve-hour day. Senior's absurd claim that the capitalist's profit was produced in the last (twelfth) hour of the working day was worthy only of an apologist for the system. Marx has no hesitation in regarding Senior as the most vulgar of political economists, and an ideologist in the worst possible sense.[25]

More recently, the Italian Marxist Antonio Gramsci (1891-1937) has developed, with his concept of hegemony, Marx's notion that the ruling ideology in an epoch is the ideology of the ruling class. Gramsci distinguishes between two forms of exercising political power. Political power can be exercised most obviously by employing physical means. The majority can be cowed into the acceptance of power through the open use of state force. Means for deploying such force exist in all societies: the police, armed forces, prisons and courts of law. However, just as important, in Gramsci's view, as the open, physical means are the cultural, ideological means. A society's stability is maintained, in his opinion, as much through the promulgation of ideas favourable to the ruling group as through the explicit (or implicit) threat of the use of force. Gramsci employs the term hegemony to describe the domination exercised by the modern state so as to emphasize the cultural, intellectual dimension of the control.

What is particularly interesting about Gramsci's account of hegemony is that he sees intellectual and cultural control in modern society as being deployed by a far larger group than apparently conceived by Marx and Engels. As well as the more normal channels of the communication of ideas, through newspapers, books and journals, Gramsci argues that there is a direct dimension of influence in the workplace, through the control over ideas exercised by foremen, supervisors and managers. Gramsci has his eye here on the growth of a technical élite who come to dominate the thinking of the ordinary person not so much through their conventional, intellectual qualifications as through their skilled expertise. As he puts it, 'In the modern world, technical education, closely bound to industrial labour even at the most primitive and unqualified level, must form the basis of the new type of intellectual.'[26]

With Gramsci, the Marxian notion that intellectual supremacy flows from material supremacy in society takes on a wider and new perspective. In Marx and Engel's conception there appears to be no great merit nor intrinsic worth in the intellectual dominance exercised by the ruling group. Gramsci's account seems, on the other hand, to suggest that the dominance may have some justification, albeit within the terms of production as currently organized. Thus Gramsci would have the subordinate masses not so much being wholly misled and confused by the communicative and intellectual frame of reference of the élite but partially so. Gramsci is prepared to concede to the technical élite under capitalism that, as things are currently constituted, they probably know best how to organize production.

This points to the element of consent involved in the acceptance of the ideology of the ruling groups by the masses. It is wrong to think of the ordinary person as being totally vulnerable to a wholly alien ideology. In the absence of an attainable alternative the ruling ideas may well make limited sense to the ordinary person. It may well be possible for a member of the British working class to lead a more normal adjusted life, for instance, by accepting the right of the royal family to be sovereign. Most certainly, in the context of factory production, to accept the organizing ideas of the supervisor and manager would make for an easier life for the ordinary worker. Thus, in relation to the dominating ideas of the ruling group, it may well be wrong to regard the thinking of the worker as entirely passive. The worker may voluntarily embrace those social, political and economic ideas in the absence of other, more practical, ones.

This is a point brought out by Lenin in his essay *What is to be done?* He makes a great deal of the fact that the thinking of workers is strongly imbued with bourgeois ideology. However, Lenin's concept of ideology needs to be carefully distinguished from that of Marx and Engels. Lenin, unlike Marx and Engels, sees all forms of social thinking as being inherently ideological. For Lenin the choice one has to make in present-day society reduces itself to a choice between bourgeois and proletarian socialist ideology. Lenin is, though, in no doubt as to which is the predominant ideology, even amongst members of the working class. Members of the working class are unfortunately steeped in bourgeois ideology. They are often monarchists where they should be republicans, they often favour radical individualism where they should be more communitarian in spirit. This is why in Lenin's view, one cannot rely on the natural, spontaneous tendencies of the working class. As he famously puts it, 'the history of all countries shows that the working class, solely by its own forces, is able to work out merely trade-union consciousness, that is, the conviction of the need for combining in unions, for fighting against the employers, and for trying to prevail upon the government to pass laws necessary for the workers'.[27]

So socialist theory has to come to the working class from the outside. Historically, socialist theorists have been members of the bourgeoisie. Marx and Engels themselves were members of the educated middle classes. Unfortunately the natural ideology of members of the working class is bourgeois ideology. The spontaneous growth of their movement will lead only to their adopting bourgeois doctrines in a modified form. For Lenin there is a quite simple answer to the question 'Why does the spontaneous movement of the working class lead to the domination of bourgeois thinking?' The simple reason is that 'bourgeois ideology is far older in origin than the socialist ideology, because it is more completely developed, and because it possesses immeasurably greater means for being spread'.[28]Workers embrace bourgeois ideology quite simply because they feel most at home with it.

Marx makes no bones about the revolutionary nature of his theory of ideology. Ideology is an inheritance of the class-divided societies of the past and present. Ideology is deep-seated. The errors such a form of thought contains cannot be removed nor its hold over the population be undermined without the complete social order to which the ideology belongs being overturned. For instance, people really only cease to believe in the ideology of the divine right of kings when not only has the idea been theoretically criticized but also when kings have actually been overthrown. Marx makes the same point trenchantly in his criticism of Feuerbach's attitude to religion in his *Theses on Feuerbach*.

Feuerbach starts out from the fact of religious self-alienation, the dupli-cation of the world into a religious and secular world. His work consists in resolving the religious world into its secular basis. But the fact that the secular basis becomes separate from itself and establishes an independent realm in the clouds can only be explained by the cleavage and self-contradic-tions of the secular basis. Thus the latter must itself be both understood in its contradiction and revolutionized in practice. For instance, after the earthly family is found to be the secret of the holy family, the former must then be theoretically and practically nullified.[29]

The criticism of an ideology is not enough, the criticism has to be followed through in revolutionary practice.

CRITICISM OF MARX'S THEORY

The major criticism that can be made of Marx's theory of ideology is that it is ambiguous and therefore confusing. The ambiguity arises from the fact that there appear to be two different versions of Marx's theory. There is the predominant view, which I have dealt with earlier, that ideology represents some kind of unavoidable misunderstanding of our real cir-cumstances, and a somewhat contrary view which can be elicited from other of Marx's comments, principally the 1859 Preface to *Contribution to the Critique of Political Economy*, that ideology is simply the intellectual climate which arises at a certain stage in the development of society.[30] In the 1859 Preface Marx argues that we should distinguish between the economic or material basis of society, namely those forces and relations of production which make human social life possible and the society's cultural, legal and political forms. Marx argues that the major changes in society occur first through an alteration in the material basis of society and suggests that 'in studying such transformations it is always necessary to distin-guish between the material transformation of the economic conditions of production, which can be determined with the precision of natural science, and the legal, political, religious, artistic or philosophical—in short, ideological forms in which men become conscious of this conflict and fight it out'.[31] Here Marx appears to use the term 'ideological forms' in a more neutral sense than he uses the term when criticizing his opponents in political economy and philosophy. As Marx employs the term here it would appear that everyone involved in the production of ideas is involved in producing ideology. This conclusion, of course, runs contrary to his own critical or negative theory of ideology.

Some justification for Marx's position in the Preface might be given by suggesting that Marx had in mind the prevailing intellectual forms of his own time and not necessarily all intellectual forms when using the term ideology. There is no doubt that Marx believed that the dominant religious, artistic, legal, cultural and social ideas of his time were ideological in the negative sense. They were both the prevailing ideas *and* largely incorrect. But Marx does not make this sufficiently explicit for even his best-known followers. Here confusion and ambiguity reign.

Barth in his important book *Truth and Ideology* points out that Marx has at least partially to exclude natural science and mathematics from the realm of ideology.[32] There is no doubt that Marx would hope to see his own scientific method as free from ideological distortion. Thus a general formulation, such as might be elicited from the 1859 Preface, which regards all the thinking of a period as ideological must lead Marx into difficulties. It is not surprising therefore that Lenin consistently used the term ideology in the sense of a doctrine reflecting the circumstances of a group, and even spoke of 'correct' Marxist ideology. Although it is inconceivable that Marx could speak in terms of a 'correct' ideology, given his negative theory, none the less Marx lays himself open to such an interpretation through some of his remarks on ideology.

Thus, Lenin's use of the term does follow one possible reading of Marx and Engel's thinking. Just as bourgeois society gives rise to a distinctive ideology of its own: the ideology of its ruling class—which Marx often refers to as 'bourgeois ideology'—so socialist society will give rise to an ideology of its own. Lenin anticipates the development of socialist society by referring to the thinking of its dominant class as 'working class ideology'. Indeed Lenin sees it as an important part of the preparatory battle of a socialist party in a capitalist society to see off the rival ideology of the bourgeoisie. In this respect the ambiguity in Marx's account of ideology paves the way for more radical interpretations of his doctrine. Whereas Marx and Engel's predominant view appears to be that there is no such thing as 'good' ideology, with Lenin 'bad' ideology must make room for the 'good'. Like the bourgeoisie, the proletariat must develop its own ideological leaders.[33]

A further difficulty with Marx's theory of ideology may arise if one regards the economic forces conditioning the intellectual and cultural superstructure of society in the broadest possible sense. On one reading, Marx means by the economic basis of society not only its technical forces of production but also the social relations of production. But it might be argued that all human relations to things and to other individuals fall under this category. The relation between a writer and his public, a priest and his confessant, the nurse and patient, husband and wife, parents and children are all also economic relations. Thus Marx's proposition would simply be that everybody's thinking is conditioned by their predominant activity. But then there appears to be no category of non-economic relations to be influenced by economic relations. All our thinking, so it seems, has economic connotations. Thus a sceptic might argue that any theory, such as Marx's, which explains *part* of the content of all our thinking is so general as to be of little value in explaining the particular ideas that are expressed. At one level, the assertion that our thinking is related to our activity appears so trivial as hardly to be worth mentioning.

This is a criticism the proponent of Marx's theory of ideology cannot avoid. Marx's theory is a general theory which regards all thinking as economically conditioned. What we do strongly conditions what we think. Some may see this as so vague and general an assertion that they feel unable to accept it as a legitimate theory. However, what the Marxian might say in defence of the view is that the general proposition evinces itself in an infinite variety of ways, so the economic dimension to a particular line of argument has always to be thought through in any specific instances of ideological discussion. The statements of a priest about his role as a confessor, the statements of parents about their role as parents, that of authors about their relations with their audience have to be connected in each instance with the particular relation of production and distribution at issue. Thus, Marx's theory of ideology should not be seen as an explanation of every form of human thought but as a prospectus about how we might go about understanding any particular instance of human thinking. There is much more to human practical activity, especially work and labour, than first meets the eye. Because economic determination is such a universal feature of our thought, it cannot preclude the possibility that such 'determined' thinking may express elements of what is true.

It is also possible to question Marx's account of the role that the division of labour plays in giving rise to ideology. On the basis of Marx's own account one might easily argue that either ideology caused by the division of labour is unavoidable or that ideology is not brought about by the division of labour *per se*. Needless to say, these are contradictory conclusions. The first conclusion might be drawn on the basis of Marx's assertion that ideology originates in the division between mental and physical labour, and the second might be drawn on the basis of Marx's claim that it is the *capitalist* division of labour that leads to opacity in the comprehension of our social relations.

If ideology is occasioned by the division between mental and physical labour it would seem that ideology in some measure must be found in all societies. The only society where it is possible to envisage mental labour and physical labour merging into one another is a primitive one in which all labour is strenuous and physical. In all other societies some individuals are going to be more occupied than others in intellectual activity. Marx and Engel's suggestion in *German Ideology* that in a communist society specilization would be set to one side is, therefore, an unrealistic one. Experience appears to prove that there are always some individuals who are more skilled than others at certain activities. Individuals may want to dabble at a variety of activities, but any rational society will encourage individuals to involve themselves most in the activities at which they are best. Following this argument, we have to conclude that there will always be some individuals who will be relatively more occupied by intellectual activities and will, therefore, hold a distinctively intellectual position in society.

If Marx and Engel's suggestion is, therefore, that the division between mental and physical labour always gives rise to ideology, we must conclude that ideology is inherent in society. This is clearly contrary to their view that ideology can in the end be overcome. But it can plausibly be argued that Marx and Engels are not suggesting that the division between mental and physical labour always causes ideology but, rather, that the historical inception of the division gave an important impetus to the development of ideology. It is not the division between the two forms of labour that allows ideology to gain a hold but the supposition that only those who are allotted the task of intellectual labour are qualified to think and theorize. Marx and Engels, in the tradition of the Enlightenment, want everyone to think for themselves and this, they suggest, may help undermine ideology.

Although Marx and Engels may escape the suggestion that their view of the role of the division of labour in the development of ideology implies ideology is inevitable, they will have greater difficulty in avoiding the criticism that on one reading their view implies that it is not the division of labour *per se* which gives rise to ideology. They are guilty of confusing this issue. They appear not to be sure whether the division of labour causes ideology or is merely a contributory factor. The second aspect of their attack on the division of labour is to suggest that such a division is to be found in present-day society and this division necessarily gives rise to misunderstandings and confusion in the minds of ordinary individuals. Marx and Engels are speaking here, of course, of the *capitalist* division of labour. The capitalist division of labour is, they complain, wholly unplanned. Its effects force themselves on the individual worker in a natural way. To lose one's job, to have one's wages cut and to be made temporarily idle are things which force themselves upon individual workers almost as acts of nature. An individual worker may think himself the cause of his decline when in fact his performance may always have been excellent. Such thinking Marx and Engels would regard as being ideologically distorted. But, in blaming the capitalist division of labour, Marx and Engels insufficiently distinguish between the confusion caused by specialization brought about by market demands and the specialization that would be necessary in any society to maintain a high level of productivity. They wrongly imply that getting rid of ideology as they understand it would also mean getting rid of specialization. This is despite the fact that the gist of their own argument is that it is not specialization in itself that leads to distortion but, rather, capitalist specialization. It seems some forms of specialization would be necessary, even desirable, in a society which planned its production.

A final criticism that may be made of Marx's approach is that his solution to the ideological distortion of our thinking appears too drastic. Many may accept his explanation of ideology, but few will be inclined to accept that the only satisfactory way to rid society of ideology is through social revolution. Even if persuaded that this is the only effective solution, many would question if the upheaval were justified. Taking a pessimistic view of human capabilities, we might suggest that there will always be those who will live in ignorance and confusion. Why should we disturb the well-being of the majority so that the discontented few can see and understand society properly? This is, of course, a criticism of the Promethean spirit which underlies Marx's revolutionary thinking. Marx does not fear stealing fire from the gods and putting it, for better or ill, in the hands of humankind. Those of a less intrepid nature will always question the value of shedding too much light on our condition and so trying to set it right.

NOTES

1. *Writings of the Young Marx on Philosophy and Society*, edited and translated by L. D. Easton and K. H. Guddat, Doubleday Anchor, New York, 1967, p.415.
2. *ibid.* p.409.
3. K. Marx, *Contribution to the Critique of Political Economy*, Lawrence & Wishart, London, 1971, p.20.

4.   L. D. Easton and K. H. Guddat (eds), *op. cit.* p.409.
5.   *ibid.* p.409.
6.   *ibid.* p.414.
7.   *ibid.* p.414.
8.   *ibid.* p.414.
9.   *ibid.* p.414.
10. *ibid.* p.414.
11. *ibid.* p.415.
12. R. Berki and B. Parekh (eds), *Knowledge and Belief in Politics*, Allen & Unwin, London, 1973, p.57.
13. L. D. Easton and K. H. Guddat (eds), *op cit.* p.423.
14. *ibid.* p.424.
15. K. Marx, *Capital*, Vol. 1, Lawrence & Wishart, London, 1970, p.106.
16. L. D. Easton and K. H. Guddat (eds), *op. cit.* p.425.
17. K. Marx, *Capital*, Vol. 1, p.80.
18. L. D. Easton and K. H. Guddat (eds), *op. cit.* p.432.
19. K. Marx, *Capital*, Vol. 1, p.75.
20. L. D. Easton and K. H. Guddat (eds), *op. cit.* pp.432-3.
21. *ibid.* p.433.
22. K. Marx and F. Engels, *Selected Works in One Volume*, London, 1969, p.35.
23. L. D. Easton and K. H. Guddat (eds), *op. cit.* p.438.
24. *ibid.* p.438.
25. K. Marx, *Capital*, Vol. 1., pp.596-7, note 3.
26. Gramsci, *Selections from the Prison Notebooks*, Lawrence & Wishart, London, 1971, p.9.
27. V. I. Lenin, *What is to be done?*, Panther, Oxford University Press, 1970, p.80.
28. *ibid.* pp.90-1.
29. L. D. Easton and K. H. Guddat (eds), *op. cit.* p.401.
30. *Contribution to the Critique of Political Economy*, Lawrence & Wishart, London, 1971, pp.20-1.
31. *ibid.* p.21.
32. K. Barth, *Truth and Ideology*, University of California Press, Los Angeles, 1976.
33. Cf. J. Larrain, *Marxism and Ideology*, Macmillan, London, 1983, pp.64-65.

2 Karl Mannheim on Ideology

Mannheim's fundamental thesis on ideology is similar to that of Marx. In Mannheim's view all human knowledge is socially conditioned. He makes a great deal of the fact that in every period in human history there exists 'representative' ideas: ideas which express the prevailing social climate. We are all bound to the climate of our times in an unavoidable way. This is a view similar to that expressed by the philosopher Hegel who says in his *Philosophy of Right* that each individual is 'a child of his time' and we can no more leap beyond our time than an individual could proverbially, in Greek times, leap over Rhodes.[1] Like many theorists of ideology Mannheim was influenced by Hegel's historical approach to human consciousness, outlined by Hegel in such works as *Phenomenology of Spirit* and *Encyclopaedia of Philosophical Sciences*. Mannheim expands this historical approach into a relativist view of all our thinking which sees our thinking as true only in respect to the time and circumstances within which it is found. According to him, even the scholar's own reasoning does not escape this relativism. His only advantage over the man in the street is that through the 'sociology of knowledge' he can become aware of the social forces which lie behind his own thinking.

The Particular and Total Conceptions of Ideology
Mannheim believes it is most important to distinguish between the 'particular' and 'total' conceptions of ideology. The first represents a primarily individual, psychological explanation of the phenomenon of ideology, and the second repre-

sents a full sociological and cultural explanation of the phenomenon.

The particular conception of ideology operates at the level of individual awareness. It is often used when dealing with the argument of an especially stubborn opponent. We cease trying to understand the argument in the opponent's terms and try to look for other less obvious explanations for his/her position. We may suspect our opponent is lying and we begin to see his or her ideas 'as more or less conscious disguises of the real nature of a situation, the true recognition of which would not be in accord with his or her interests'.[2] Instead of seeing our intellectual opponent's arguments simply in a logical and deductive sense we begin to look at those arguments in relation to what the individual is. We see them not only in the light of the reasoning they display but also as expressions of the nature of the individual's existence and character.

We begin to attribute to the individual *motives* (as opposed to reasons) for holding to his or her position. We suggest, for instance, the opponent will not acknowledge this or that statement to be true because it is not in his or her interests to do so. Our adversary will ignore certain facts because they do not fit in with the interests he or she is defending. This *particular* conception of ideology looks upon the individual in a *utilitarian* way. Every individual, it is agreed, in pursuit of self-interest will interpret the facts according to his or her needs at the time. Should it suit them, people will acknowledge their needs and interests in their entirety; but our minds are so constituted that if an element of the facts runs counter to our requirements we will ignore it. So *part* of what the individual says is taken to be misleading because it disguises his or her true interests. Here the connection with psychology and Freud's notion of the unconscious is striking. In Freud's psychology it is taken for granted that individuals suppress aspects of what is the case in order to protect the integrity of their personality.

Mannheim is quick to point out what he thinks are the defects of this *particular* view of ideology. He thinks its prime defect is that it focuses entirely upon the individual. In its simplest form, this view of ideology suggests that its cause is selfishness or egotism. The individual, it suggests, ignores all that it is convenient for him or her not to see. Mannheim especially objects to the application of the particular conception of ideology to the thinking of groups. A reductionist approach such as this, which breaks up each group into a number of individuals motivated by self-interest, entirely misjudges the nature of ideology. Such an approach does not explain the phenomenon of ideology; it is merely another way of identifying its existence. What has to be explained is why individuals find it necessary to clothe their self-interest with illusions and deceptions? For Mannheim, ideology is not merely a psychological phenomenon occuring in the individual's mind, it is part of a more deep-lying social condition.

It is to counter the weakness of the particular, psychological view of ideology that Mannheim puts forward his total conception of ideology. There are a number of aspects of the total view which are shared with the particular view. The total view, like the particular view, does not rely solely on what others say to interpret their meaning and intention. Secondly, both views look at the social condition of others to explain their position, although the emphasis on the group situation in the total view is far greater. So, thirdly, both look on the ideas of others as a function of their existence. However,

Whereas the particular conception of ideology designates only a part of the opponent's assertions as ideologies—the total conception calls into question the opponent's total *Weltanschauung* (including his conceptual apparatus) and attempts to understand these concepts as an outgrowth of the collective life of which he partakes.[3]

The total conception of ideology does not leave a stone unturned in its determination to get at the truth. It not only brings into question the individual's underlying assumptions but also the underlying assumptions of the culture of the social group to which the individual belongs. The total conception of ideology requires the use of a radically different technique from the particular conception. With the particular conception it is still assumed that both the analyst and the ideologist share a common fund of knowledge which provides criteria acceptable to both for judging the truth or falsity of an argument. With the particular conception it is still assumed possible to use this common belief to show to the victim of ideology the error of his or her ways.

But this is not so with the total conception of ideology. The assumptions of the analyst are fundamentally different from those of his subject. In the first place, 'the total conception uses' a 'formal fundamental analysis, without any reference to *motivation*'.[4] Concentration on a psychology of interests is replaced by a concentration upon objective social and economic circumstances. What are crucial here are not subjective inclinations or feelings but the effect of social settings upon an individual's perspectives. Thus, secondly, 'as soon as the total conception of ideology is used, we attempt to reconstruct *the whole outlook of a social group*, and neither the concrete individuals nor the abstract sum of them can legitimately be considered as bearers of this ideological thought system as a whole'. 'The aim of the analysis at this level is the reconstruction of the systematic theoretical basis underlying the single judgements of the individual.'[5]

So Mannheim sees ideologies as operating through individuals and groups, rather than individuals and groups creating them in response to their circumstances. Both the personality of the individual and the personality of the group is formed by the collective ideology. In this respect Mannheim is more mechanistic in his view of ideology than Marx. Ideological thinking, Mannheim suggests, comes to the individual from the outside. It is likely that the individual will grasp no more than a fragment of the ideology as a whole. The ideology as a whole is a product of the group's *collective* unconscious. And the task of the analyst of ideologies is to unmask the influence which the collective unconscious has upon our thinking. Whereas the particular conception of ideology only betrays an attitude of mistrust towards the opinions and doctrines of others, the total conception of ideology revolutionizes our attitudes to the opinions and doctrines of others. We see individuals in the light of these 'total' social historical settings. Because this revolutionary change applies to the analyst as well as other individuals, it raises a profound problem about *thought* in general.

But if all consciousness is socially and historically conditioned, it is possible to have knowledge at all? Mannheim does not have a fully satisfactory answer to this problem. However, he argues that it is in the nature of the case that there can be no satisfactory answer. For him this problem lies at the core of a new discipline he would like to invent, namely the sociology of knowledge. The sociology of knowledge would see each and every one of our ideas and conceptions as the necessary outgrowth of our collective unconscious. 'Underlying even the profound insight of the genius are the collective historical experiences of a group which the individual takes for granted.'[6]

Here we see for the first time Mannheim's thoroughgoing relativism. What is meant by relativism is the rejection of all absolute criteria of truth. Mannheim stresses that 'as long as one does not call his own position into question but regards it as absolute, while interpreting his opponents' ideas as a mere function of the social positions they occupy, the decisive step forward has not been taken'.[7] To be successful, ideological analysis not only has to subject the adversary's point of view but 'all points of view', including its own to socio-historical observation. This would, in Mannheim's view, distinguish his method from the Marxist analysis of ideologies. Marxists are wedded to one world view as the correct one. This prevents them from seeing the relatedness of all historically developed systems of thought, including their own.

But Mannheim denies his view is relativist. He describes it rather as relationist.[8] And his thesis is that all historical knowledge is relational knowledge. The person who analyses ideologies cannot escape from the historical basis of his own thinking. He stresses that 'we need not regard it as a source of error that all thought is so rooted'.[9] However, in analysing ideologies, the analyst should seek to avoid making value judgements and to present the social context in which a particular system of ideas and doctrines arises in as clear a light as possible. Above all, Mannheim wants to avoid the student of ideology taking a superior attitude in relation to the ideologies being examined. We are all enmeshed in the thinking of our age and there is no eagle-like position of flight which allows a vantage point over all ideologies.

Because the analyst cannot himself but be influenced by the ideologies he is studying, this should not lead him to despair of arriving at knowledge. Intimate acquaintance with things often gives rise to the most profound insights. Provided we are aware of the hold that ideas have on the individuals we are studying, we can add to our own knowledge. In seeing the intimate connection between circumstances and ideas we become more sceptical of our most cherished beliefs, just as we do of the beliefs of others. This scepticism is a form of knowledge.

Knowledge, as seen in the light of the total conception of ideology, is by no means an illusory experience, for ideology in its relational concept is not at all identical with illusion. Knowledge arising out of our experience in actual life situations, though not absolute, is knowledge none the less.[10]

What we should aim at is a more comprehensive view than that of those who are actively involved in expounding ideologies. We know the conclusions we come to are limited by our own social and historical horizons, but they have a better chance of being appropriate than non-analytical views. We can be satisfied that what we know is knowledge for that *time*. It may well cease to be relevant when society changes, but this will present the sociology of knowledge with a new task. Knowledge appears to the sociologist of knowledge as an ever-recurring challenge rather than a number of fixed conclusions which are valid for all time. We have to learn to think 'dynamically and relationally rather than statically'.[11]

So Mannheim's theory of ideology provides knowledge which is true for the period in history of which it is part. It sees the structural causes of social and political disputes and it can weigh the opposing arguments against the underlying situation. For this reason it can see which political action and solutions are possible and those which are entirely out of tune with the times. Political science must reject such anachronistic conclusions. Its task, is, therefore, to criticize systems of thinking which prevent individuals from adjusting to the times in which they live. Political science has to point out the 'antiquated norms' and confused systems of thought that prevent proper 'acclimatizations'. Thus, the political doctrine which emerges from Mannheim's theory of ideology is, then, one of 'adjustment'. Mannheim believes that the individual from the point of view of his social health should aim at coming to terms, partially at least, with the society in which he lives.

Mannheim, as we have seen, claims his view of ideology does not rest on a relativist view of truth. I think he is wrong to do so. His relativism becomes apparent when he advocates a compromise view of what we are aiming at in the social sciences. *He suggests we should set as our goal the adjustment of individuals to their historical circumstances.* Now, although he admits that these are historically changing circumstances, he must acknowledge he is asking the individual to accept some of the parameters of the society as more or less ideal. Once he implies in his analysis that certain social parameters are ideal he undermines his view of relationist truth. According to him, these 'ideals' will change from age to age. So the recommendations of the sociology of knowledge itself must change from age to age. Is this not another form of relativism? In asking the good citizen and the sociologist of knowledge continually to adjust to a moving target, he leaves them without any solid foundation on which to build their view of the world. Any theory which is not wholly relative must rest on some permanent criteria of worth and truth. Such criteria are to be found, for instance, in the work of philosophers such as Kant, who, in his moral philosophy, presents a notion of a 'kingdom of ends' which must underlie any society where ethical harmony is to be attained. For Mannheim's relationist theory to work, he must stipulate what forms of 'adjustment' he favours. He would have to outline a notion of a community where the attainment of moral ideals is possible. This he fails to do. This failure is apparent in his account of the intellectual and society and the distinction he makes between ideology and Utopia.

The intellectual and society

Mannheim stresses the *relative* autonomy of the intellectual within society. He makes use of the phrase (coined by A. Weber) *Freischwebende Intelligenz*, or 'free-floating intellectual', to convey this idea.[12] The intellectual and intellectuals as a whole are a microcosm of society. In them the competing forces and movements of society coalesce. Intellectuals are drawn from different class backgrounds (albeit that they are predominantly middle class) and their common educational concerns drown sectarian aspirations.

Side by side with the development of this disinterested group, society becomes, Mannheim suggests, more subject to the 'flow of ideas'. Intellectual activity is not limited to the privileged few: everybody believes they have the right to their say. Of course, the intellectual can always choose to attach himself/herself to one or two of the warring camps in society, but there is no doubt what Mannheim's choice is. Intellectuals must, he suggests, become aware of the 'mission implicit' in their peculiar social position.[13] They must strive for a total perspective.[14] 'Thus they might play the part of watchmen in what otherwise would be a pitch-black night.'[15] To do this, intellectuals have to accomplish a task not demanded of any other class in society. Firstly, they have to try to step aside from any material goals they may wish to set themselves so that, secondly, they might see things in their truth. Mannheim doubtlessly believes that only a few intellectuals are capable of attaining or even approximating to this goal, but he is sufficiently optimistic to think that some may. The role that Mannheim sets intellectuals is reminiscent of the task given to philosopher kings in Plato's *Republic*. Plato believes that it is possible to train a class of individuals who will excel both in physical skills and intellectual attributes. Through their intellectual abilities they will be able to see what is best for society and, in order that they see their interests only in terms of the community as a whole, Plato intends to deprive them of private property. Mannheim does not go to these lengths in outlining the class of 'free-floating intellectuals' he would like to see. His vision of the role of the intellectual in society is perhaps nearer to the role that Hegel sees what he calls the 'universal class' playing in his *Philosophy of Right*.[16] For Hegel, this universal class is the most important social group in modern society. Those who belong to this class are civil servants, priests, lawyers and teachers: in short, all those who belong to callings for which intellectual qualifications are essential. This universal class clearly has close affinities with Mannheim's notion of the free-floating intelligentsia, since the political role of members of this class is to safeguard the interests of the whole society in an unbiased way.

For Mannheim the possibility of politics as a science arises from the potential neutrality of the intelligentsia. Members of the intelligentsia are aware of all the conflicting movements, yet they are fully committed to none. Such free-floating intellectuals do not wish to get rid of the normative side of politics because this is precisely the stuff from which politics is made: conflicts about norms. The role of such intellectuals should be to make the participants more aware of the origins of their interests and concerns, and those of their opponents. Mannheim is therefore against the intellectual taking sides in a narrow party political sense; however, he is not against the intellectual taking a practical stance so long as the goal is that of progress.

Ideology and Utopia

For Mannheim 'a state of mind is Utopian when it is incongruous with the state of reality within which it occurs'.[17] This is a necessary condition for the Utopian frame of mind to exist but it is not sufficient. For not every frame of mind which seeks to transcend the existing order is Utopian, only that frame of mind which also breaks the bonds of the present state of affairs. Here there arises a distinction between Utopian frameworks and ideological frameworks. Ideological states of mind are very often 'incongruent with reality' but they can be made harmless, that is, not subversive. Indeed there are such things, according to Mannheim, 'as appropriate ideologies' for a stage of existence.

Thus both Utopias and ideologies are not in tune with the reality which they partially reflect. Mannheim attributes this lack of harmony in both instances to the collective unconscious of the groups involved. With the Utopian mentality, on the one hand, what the collective unconscious suppresses are those aspects of reality which might permanently stand in the way of the group attaining its goal. With the ideological standpoint, what the collective unconscious suppresses are, on the other hand, those facts which might tend to undermine the stability of the established order.

Furthermore, Mannheim associates ideologies and Utopias with two diametrically opposed forms of social group. Utopias arise where 'certain oppressed groups are intellectually so strongly interested in the destruction and transformation of a given condition of society that they unwittingly see only those elements in the situation which tend to negate it'.[18] Utopias are, therefore, associated with the lower end of the social scale. Ideologies are, in contrast, associated with the upper end of the social scale. They occur because 'ruling groups can in their thinking become so intensively interest-bound to a situation that they are simply no longer able to see certain facts which would undermine their sense of domination'.[19]

Christian ideas in feudal society were primarily ideological. The teachings of the Catholic Church on divine authority chimed in well with the apparent absolute authority of monarchs and lords. Christianity fitted in well with the period so long as its critical ideas were located in another world. It was only when certain sects tried to put those ideas into practice that they became Utopian. From this point of view, 'Ideologies are the situationally transcendent ideas which never succeed *de facto* in the realization of their projected contents.'[20] There is something inherently unreal about ideologies—take the Christian view of brotherly love—but despite or perhaps because of their unreality they often perform a stabilizing task.

Utopias are not ideologies, Mannheim suggests, 'in the measure and in so far as they succeed through counteractivity in transforming the existing historical reality into one more in accord with their own conceptions'.[21] Thus in so far as individuals or groups are successful in carrying out the aim of their ideology those individuals or groups are Utopian. But Mannheim does point out that ruling groups at all times have claimed that ideas of rebellious groups are Utopian, even where the ideas of these groups have not in fact represented the society of the future. Ruling classes have, on the whole, failed to distinguish between Utopias and ideologies, and, for the most part, have even profited from their confusion. It is not in the interest of ruling classes to distinguish between ideas that may one day be realized and ideas that can never be realized. Ruling classes would prefer to see all such 'reality transcending ideas as unrealizable or Utopian'.[22] We must, however, try to avoid this one-sidedness in the use of the term *Utopian*, because every age gives rise, in Mannheim's view, to its Utopia 'in which are continued in condensed form the unrealized and the unfulfilled tendencies which represent the needs' of the age.[23] The role of the 'free-floating intellectual' in the present day is to try to discover what those unfulfilled tendencies and needs are now.

The Utopia of the ascendant middle class in the eighteenth and nineteenth centuries was the doctrine of 'freedom'.[24] With the benefit of historical hindsight, we can see there were many of what Mannheim would call 'real elements' in this Utopia; that is, the doctrine was not wholly ideological. Freedom of employment, freedom of place of residence, freedom of conscience and speech; all these were great advances when they were realized, if only for the minority. In their conception of Utopia the middle class were not wholly deceiving themselves and others. There was a better future at which their ideas were aiming. And indeed this is a feature of Utopias, according to Mannheim; that they are more socially progressive than ideologies. Ideologies generally serve to *mask* the existing order whereas Utopias do contain ideas which can be 'adequately realized in the succeeding social order'.[25] For this reason it is much easier to distinguish ideologies and Utopias *retrospectively*.

Mannheim himself acknowledges that it is very difficult in practice to distinguish between ideologies and Utopias.[26] The existing powers will necessarily label as Utopian what goes beyond the 'preservation of their interests'. But the blanket condemnation does not serve to identify those ideas which will allow society to develop from its present state. Mannheim suggests we should look at society 'dialectically' to decide what are the real 'Utopias', that is, the ideas which have a chance of being realized. Utopias for Mannheim (quoting Lamartine), 'are often only premature truths'.[27] Just as ascendant social groups unmask the anachronistic ideologies of the existing order, so dominant groups unmask the premature 'Utopias' of the future.

We learn why Mannheim thinks it so difficult to distinguish between Utopias and ideologies when he speaks of their role in history. He claims that when we can, in retrospect, see that ideas were merely a 'distorted representation' of a part or potential social order we can say with precision that they were ideological. However, other ideas which appeared to be out of tune with their time but were subsequently realized institutionally can with certainty be called Utopian. Thus it is only practice or the historical evolution of the human species which distinguishes the two. 'If we look into the past,' he says, 'it seems possible to find a fairly adequate criterion of what is to be regarded as ideological and what as Utopian. This criterion is their realization.'[28] At the time we cannot know with certainty which ideas are going to turn out be ideological and which are going to turn out to be Utopian; the future only will tell.

It appears that Mannheim's theory of ideology has a great deal in common with psychoanalytic theory—very much the vogue in the Germany of Mannheim's youth. Mannheim's goal appears to be the intellectual health of the community. Just as the psychoanalyst's goal is to divert the mental patient's thinking away from his private world to an adjustment with the everyday world, Mannheim's goal appears to be to make the collective entity-society adjust to the reality of its circumstances. Like the psychoanalyst, Mannheim recognizes that that world in which we live is not in any sense an ultimate one—since it is always subject to alteration and improvement, he none the less recommends swimming with the tide. All is well if we can assume this tide is a progressive one, but difficulties unavoidably arise once we realize that the future direction of society is an open-ended one. Just as with the psychoanalyst involved in therapy, Mannheim may be asking his patient to adjust to a fundamentally unhealthy society.

CRITICISMS OF MANNHEIM'S APPROACH TO IDEOLOGY

I have already anticipated some criticisms in my account of Mannheim's theory of ideology. I have suggested, firstly, that Mannheim fails properly to distinguish between his relationist view of knowledge and the relativist view; secondly, that his relationist view places the supposed 'free-floating intellectual' in an untenable position; finally, that the politics of adjustment which flows from this account of ideology need not necessarily be a healthy one.

There is not complete agreement amongst philosophers as to what the term relativism stands for; however, it is generally used to suggest that all knowledge gains its status from the standpoint of one individual (or group of individuals) in particular. Knowledge is relative to the standpoint of the percipient or subject. A consequence of this view is that it is possible to have conflicting accounts of what is true. What is true for you or the social group to which you belong may well not be true for another person or social group. What is regarded as knowledge can vary both from the standpoint of time and place. Thus, a relativist holds that there is no absolute standard of truth.

Mannheim defines relativism in historical and sociological terms. 'Relativism,' he says, 'is a product of the modern historical-sociological procedure which is based on the recognition that all historical thinking is bound up with the concrete position in life of the thinker.'[29] What Mannheim finds at fault with this view is that it leads to the conclusion that all thinking which is bound up with the subjective, historical viewpoint of an individual or group is false. It is this implication he hopes to avoid with his 'relationist' account.

However, Mannheim's adoption of the term relationism merely allows him to avoid a problem that lies at the heart of his own approach, and it is the problem of relativism.[30] Someone who takes Mannheim's relationist standpoint has still to answer why knowledge which is always perspectival and socially rooted can, none the less, be called knowledge. To call such an approach relationist is just to give the problem a different name. To make sense of his relationist viewpoint, Mannheim has to argue that there is something which characterizes all forms of knowledge offered from a relationist position as knowledge. Mannheim requires a standpoint, such as that of Kant, Marx or Wittgenstein, which acknowledges that although all knowledge is knowledge from a human perspective it nevertheless has general or universalizable properties. Relativism is not acceptable as a theory of knowledge, because the possibility even of human linguisitic communication depends on the acceptance of certain common categories and the general recognition of some utterances as true.

No linguistic communication would be possible without the recognition that some utterances within the human communicative universe must be true universally. It is possible for Mannheim to fall back on a cultural relativism which maintains that something is true only from within the standpoint of a certain society. There is no doubt that what we accept as true is coloured by our social and cultural environment. However, even the cultural relativist has to acknowledge that general or universalizable standards have to apply within that social and cultural environment; otherwise, human communication would break down.

As no such statement is forthcoming from Mannheim, his theory of ideology is bound to slip into the relativist trap. Because he puts forward no absolute conception of truth (even for our society and time) his 'free-floating intellectuals' must appear as what they no doubt are—an insulated, privileged élite. Mannheim depicts them as being 'above' the battles of everyday life and politics, seeking a superior standpoint which is relatively untarnished by practical involvement. Most individuals expect detachment from intellectuals, but what Mannheim proposes is superhuman reticence and diffidence. Mannheim does not rule our party involvement and he also recognizes that intellectuals, like all other groups, have a distinctive class position in society; but they are capable, he thinks, of withstanding all this in order to play a crucial, progressive role in society.

In short, Mannheim, like Max Weber, called on the intellectual to have a passion for science, to take science as his or her vocation, but at the same time to realize that science as a vocation was qualitatively different from politics as a vocation.[31]

The moral vision underlying this is most probably unobjectionable. Intellectuals can and should contribute towards the development of their society. But the notion that they are uniquely qualified to do so is, I think, a misplaced one. Intellectuals, in the first place, form a wider group than Mannheim suggests. The Italian Marxist, Antonio Gramsci, has, as we have seen, pointed to the markedly intellectual nature of a large number of technical jobs that are to be found in the modern market economy. He suggests that the category of intellectuals should be widened to include such people as draughtsmen, technicians, works convenors and supervisors. This is a plausible suggestion, since such people work with ideas almost as much as traditional academics and writers. In the second place, as well as making the category of intellectuals too narrow, Mannheim underestimates the amount of reflectivity of which an ordinary member of society might be capable. What Mannheim asks of intellectuals is that they exhibit self-consciousness; that they should be aware of the social and political currents of their age and understand their relationship to them. There is no reason to believe that this capability does not exist in others and, indeed, it might be plausibly held that some non-intellectuals might be capable of greater self-awareness than intellectuals. Mannheim fails properly to deal with the scepticism of the ordinary person about the peculiar standing of intellectuals. A wider view of the intelligentsia than his is called for. As three recent commentators have put it: 'It is not clear how intellectuals can be the source of a distinctive political design of their own, since they are the elaborators of all the ideologies, in the service of all social impulses'.[32]

The dubious position of Mannheim's 'free-floating intellectuals' leads one to cast doubt on the role of the science of politics that he advocates. Mannheim sees his sociology of knowledge leading to a scientific account of politics. He thinks a science of politics will allow us 'to calculate more precisely collective interests and their corresponding modes of thought and to predict approximately the ideological reactions of the different strata'.[33] No doubt reflection on any activity will allow us to comprehend more fully what is taking place but there is nothing that uniquely qualifies the political scientist for this task in the political realm. Political scientists are distinguished from the ordinary person who reflects on politics by the fact that they do so professionally—that is, they have more time to do so and are paid to do so—but there is no guarantee, as Mannheim implies, that they are better at it. It is possible to accept that the existence of departments of Political Science in universities and other institutions of higher education is likely to make the community as a whole better at political judgement, but this is not necessarily because professional political scientists exercise better judgement than others. The existence of professional political scientists draws to everyone's attention the need to make careful political judgements but it can provide no absolute guarantee that such judgement is provided. Unlike Mannheim, I do not think it is the task of political scientists to provide superior insight *per se*: their task, rather, is to encourage the development of superior political insight in others as well as in themselves. Individual political scientists may fail in this task but collectively there is sure to be some improvement.

Concern can finally be expressed about Mannheim's desire to see political scientists help political leaders in bringing about more rapid adjustment in contemporary society. As Loader aptly puts it:

The task of the political scientist was to help the politician become a relational thinker . . . This task demanded the clarification of the constellation of sociopolitical forces, the analysis of political aspirations, the imputation of their sociopolitical correlations, and the connection of theory and praxis . . . The political scientist helped the politician to develop the tools for orientation in the changing world.[34]

I have already said that political scientists are not uniquely qualified to do this. Secondly, I am not sure that for political scientists (however indirectly) to brief political leaders is the best way of tendering their advice. Any such advice is a public matter and should be tendered as widely as possible to all groups and social classes. Thirdly, it is not clear from Mannheim's sociology of knowledge to what citizens are actually to be asked to adjust. Briefly put, it appears as though Mannheim simply wants citizens open-endedly to adjust to the future.

Mannheim's overall approach might rightly be called modernist. He is hostile to outmoded political and social thought. But like most modernist thinkers he does not specify what makes a form of thought or activity outmoded. In my view this approach leaves us at the mercy of the unplanned development of history. Mannheim supposes, optimistically, that society always develops from the worse to the better. It might also be regarded as parochially pro-capitalist since the motor of historical development is in the West still the industrial and financial expansion and innovation of the advanced market economies. It is the large corporations which carry all else in their sway. Mannheim's approach suggests that, as this is the current onward direction of civilization, political scientists should do their best to ensure the world population's co-operation with it. We have to co-operate *de facto* with those who are already making the future and support those Utopias which will realize it. However, we might argue that there is no critical distance here between the observer and what is taking place in society. What ought to take place is being confused with what is taking place.

Mannheim prejudges the issue by suggesting that modernizing trends are the ones we should support. We should prepare ourselves, he thinks, for even greater modernization. But although there may be a great deal of merit in the forms of thought and society which are being shaped for us by the unplanned course of historical events, we should first pause to weigh up what is happening before giving it our uncritical support.

NOTES

1. G. W. F. Hegel, *Philosophy of Right*, Oxford University Press, 1971, p.11.
2. Mannheim, *Ideology and Utopia*, Routledge & Kegan Paul, London, 1976, p.49.
3. *ibid.* p.50.
4. *ibid.* p.51.
5. *ibid.* p.52.
6. *ibid.* p.241.
7. *ibid.* p.68.
8. C. Loader, *The Intellectual Development of Karl Mannheim*, Cambridge University Press, 1985, p.115.

   Relationism, then, meant the postponement of certainty, the commitment to a future judgement of validity. One would struggle for one's convictions, knowing they could never be universal because there was no such thing as universal validity. . . .

9. Mannheim, *op. cit.* p.71.
10. *ibid.* p.76.

11.   *ibid*. p.77.
12.   *ibid*. p.137.
13.   *ibid*. p.142.
14.   *ibid*. p.143.
15.   *ibid*. p.143.
16.   Hegel, *Philosophy of Right*, para. 205, p.132.
17.   Mannheim, *op. cit.* p.173.
18.   *ibid*. p.36.
19.   *ibid*. p.36.
20.   *ibid.* p.175.
21.   *ibid*. p.176.
22.   *ibid*. p.177.
23.   *ibid*. p.179.
24.   *ibid*. p.183.
25.   *ibid*. p.184.
26.   *ibid*. p.176.
27.   *ibid*. p.183.
28.   *ibid*. p.184.
29.   *ibid*. p.70.
30.   J. Larrain, *The Concept of Ideology*, Hutchinson, London, 1979, p.120.
31.   C. Loader, *op. cit.* p.119.
32.   Kettler, D., Meja, V., Stehr, N., *Karl Mannheim*, Ellis Horwood, London, 1985, p.58.
33.   Mannheim, op. cit. p.169.
34.   C. Loader, *op. cit.* pp.120-1.

3   The Oakeshottian View
of Ideology

By international standards, Michael Oakeshott is not a well–
known philosopher. He belongs to a philosophical school,
that of the British idealists, which is now almost extinct. The
most distinguished of these idealists were T. H. Green, F. H.
Bradley and B. Bosanquet. At the turn of the century theirs
were the leading philosophical systems of the day, and the
school had an extensive hold upon philosophy chairs in the
departments of British universities. The Scottish universities
were virtually monopolized by such lesser figures of the school
such as Caird, Henry Jones and Seth-Pringle. These British
idealists draw their inspiration from the German philosopher,
Hegel, whose writings were accepted as forming a model of
the idealist approach.

Oakeshott acknowledges his indebtedness both to Hegel
and Bradley. Oakeshott says in the introduction to his
magnum opus Experience and its Modes, 'the works from
which I am conscious of having learnt most are Hegel's
Phänomenologie des Geistes and Bradley's *Appearance and
Reality*'.[1] Both these are important works in the canon of
philosophical idealism. Oakeshott's indebtedness to Hegel is
apparent in the view that he takes of philosophy. Oakeshott
appears to be offering with this view a moderate, updated
twentieth century account of Hegel's spirit or *Geist*. Spirit of
mind is the central idea of Hegel's philosophy and it plays a
role not dissimilar to that of God in the Christian religion.
Philosophical experience, Oakeshott says, 'I take to be experience without presupposition, reservation, arrest or
modification. Philosophical knowledge is knowledge which

carries with it the evidence of its own completeness.'² *Geist*, for Hegel, is thought in its most inclusive possible sense. Hegel equally sees this *thought* as unencumbered and without presupposition.

What leads this idealist vision to a theory of ideology is the manner in which Oakeshott employs the vision to divide and separate out aspects of our experience. In the first place, philosophy for Oakeshott represents the totality of our experience. The seventeenth - century Dutch philosopher Spinoza took a similar view when he argued that *substance* represented the totality of our experience and this substance could be philosophically comprehended. But this substance, according to Spinoza, could be divided into two attributes: extension and thought. Each of these attributes then had their distinct modes which could be the subject of philosophical investigation. Oakeshott divides our experience into distinct attributes, but those attributes for him are not substantial. Since 'experience is a world of ideas',³ these attributes, or what Oakeshott calls modes, must also be worlds of ideas.

Oakeshott distinguishes four important worlds of ideas. They are the worlds of philosophy, history, science and practice. Since philosophy represents the totality of experience it necessarily stands in a superior relation to the other three. Whereas it is possible to gain a philosophical insight into, and thus supersede, the worlds of history, science and practice, it is not possible to gain a practical, historical or scientific insight into and thus supersede philosophy. Oakeshott prudently stresses that this is not an exhaustive list: 'Indeed', he says, 'there can be no limit to the number of possible modifications in experience. History, Science and Practice were selected . . . because they appeared to be the chief among the more highly organized worlds of abstract experience at the present time.'⁴

Oakeshott somewhat reverses the ordinary meaning of terms in our vocabulary when he speaks of history, practice or sciences as representing 'abstract' worlds. In his estimation, the philosophical world is the most 'concrete' or real of worlds because it takes in the totality of our experience. Other worlds can exist separately from this world, therefore, only by 'abstracting' from it. This view appears to owe something to

Hegel's claim in his *Science of Logic* that the categories and ideas with which we make sense of our experience also constitute it and are, therefore, the very essence of the world. Hegel also took the view that philosophy in the shape of his *Science of Logic* was the most concrete and real of worlds from which all else appeared an abstraction.

With Oakeshott, for something to be true requires no 'external' reference. Since all experience is an experience of ideas involving judgement, coherence provides a sufficient touchstone for determining the truth of a claim. A world of ideas is therefore established through the creation of a set of arguments which are, in their own terms, coherent. Oakeshott appears to envisage two levels of coherence. On the one hand, there is the absolute level of coherence attained only by philosophy and, on the other, there is the relative level of coherence attained by the various abstract modes of experience such as history and science.

What constitutes a coherent argument is defined within those modes of experience themselves. In Oakeshott's view, history is wholly the product of the historian. He accepts no distinction between the past thought and the past as it is in itself. Historians both create the story they tell about the past and the standards of objectivity against which the story is to be judged. The historian creates the past, but this is not the past as it is experienced by the practical person of affairs: 'History is the past for the sake of the past. What the historian is interested in is a dead past; a past unlike the present.'[5] Similarly, the world of science is constructed by scientists themselves. In their concern to unravel 'nature' they in fact create the natural world of science. Indeed, Oakeshott takes the extreme idealist view that 'Nature' as the 'mother of science' is the 'creation of the scientific mind for the sole purpose of satisfying that mind'.[6] It is scientists themselves, therefore, who determine what is objective in terms of their modes of experience. What characterizes an objective view from the scientific point of view is that the argument can be expressed in *quantitative* terms and depicts 'a world of absolutely stable and communicable experiences'.[7]

Because coherence is established only within each individual mode of experience, it follows that each mode develops a standard of truth relative only to itself:

No experience save that which belongs exclusively to its mode can help to elucidate the content of an abstract world of ideas (such as practice or history); the experience which belongs to the concrete whole (i.e. philosophy) is merely destructive of the abstract world as a world. [8]

Just as in the philosophy of Spinoza, where there is no direct access from the one attribute (*thought*) to the other (*extension*) and the connection is provided externally by God or Substance, so with Oakeshott there is no direct connection between the various modes of experience. They are drawn together only through their annihilation in philosophy. Oakeshott therefore has to go to great lengths to prove that history, science and practice do not impinge on each other. All suggestions such as that history employs scientific procedures or that science proceeds best through a historical knowledge of its own past have to be resisted. Unlike Hegel, Oakeshott also has to maintain that a knowledge of the history of philosophy has no bearing upon the activity of philosophy. In no sense can knowledge of the historical past help us with our current knowledge. We cannot transplant the knowledge gained in one mode of experience to another, for this would give rise to what Oakeshott calls an *ignoratio elenchi*.

This brings us to the distinction which Oakeshott wants to maintain above all others: the distinction between philosophy and practice. Here also lie the roots of the Oakeshottian theory of ideology. The world of practice is for Oakeshott, like all the other modes of experience, a world of ideas. Oakeshott does not accept that the practical world is a world of activity and not one of thought. Action for Oakeshott represents a particular type of thinking, that of volition; that is, thinking that provides impetus to the will. As with the other worlds of ideas, the criterion of validity is coherence. The object of our actions in the practical world is to bring greater coherence to that world; in so far as our actions succeed in that aim, they demonstrate their coherence. But this kind of coherence should not, in Oakeshott's view, be confused with historical, scientific or philosophical coherence. The truth of an idea in the practical world is far different from the truth of an idea in historical, scientific or philosophical experience.

What is unique about the practical world is that here 'the alteration of existence is undertaken'. In practice we are concerned with 'the conduct of life as such'.[9] A tension arises here between the philosophical life and the life of practice. This is because in both spheres an attempt is made to render our experience as a whole coherent. Oakeshott is intensely conscious of the rivalry between the exponent of his view of philosophy and the exponent of the primacy of practical life. Both wish to subsume the other activity. The person of practical affairs will see philosophy as a mere embellishment to our true experience, just as the philosophically inclined will see practical affairs as a mere distraction from the real world of philosophy. For the person of practical affairs, philosophy can add insight to our actions and provide a theoretical framework within which we can assess what we do, but it can never supersede the decisive area of 'the alteration of existence'.

But Oakeshott does not accept the grander claims of practice. He believes that the practical world is inherently incomplete or, in his own terms, can represent only an 'arrest' in our experience. It is only philosophy that represents experience in its unhindered totality. The rock on which practical experience founders is that of the mutability of things. Every alteration of existence is itself subject to change. There is nothing permanent in the truth which can be established in the practical world. Practical experience is active experience, and action involves change. Change inevitably implies 'a mortal world'.[10] Oakeshott sums up his view in this way:

The assertion of reality in practical judgement must remain always partial and inadequate. The presupposition of practical experience is that 'what is here and now' and 'what ought to be' are discrepant. And practice is not the reconciliation of these worlds as worlds, but the reconciliation of particular instances of this discrepancy. To reconcile these worlds . . . would involve the abolition of this discrepancy.[11]

Changing what is into what 'ought to be' is a never–ending task. So the coherence that the practical person seeks can never be fully achieved. And were it ever to be achieved it would do away with the stimulus for action. Actions can be true, therefore, only in a relative sense. There is no absolutely worthy action. The circumstances have to be right for the action to be right. Religion and morality belong *par excellence* to the practical world. Oakeshott thinks the true message of a religion lies in its recipe for the 'conduct of life' and not in its metaphysics. 'All religions are ways of living, and our religion is our way of living.'[12] But though essential to the conduct of life, religion is seen by Oakeshott—and his mentor Hegel—as an incomplete form of experience. For a totally untramelled view of experience we must turn to philosophy. An ever-changing world can never be rendered satisfactory through living one form of life.

Oakeshott proposes, then, the most radical disjuncture between philosophy and practice. 'Life', Oakeshott para-doxically asserts, 'can be conducted only at the expense of an arrest in experience.' Life detracts from philosophy, just as philosophy detracts from life. If we are actively engaged in pursuing a goal we cannot also be doing philosophy. Nothing but harm can come from the confusion and admixture of the two. Oakeshott denounces Plato's vision in the *Republic* of the philosopher ruler:

It is not the clear sighted, not those who are fashioned for thought and the ardours of thought, who can lead the world. Great achievements are accom-plished in the mental fog of practical experience. What is furthest from our needs is that kings should be philosophers.[13]

Practical life and the philosophical life are in an antagonistic relationship with one another. The price of the success of philosophy is that it should keep at bay the unseemly demands of practice. Ideology belongs to practical life and systematic (presuppositionless) thought belongs to philosophy. The true philosopher soars above the mundane world of human exis-tence; to be over-involved in its maintenance would prejudice the philosopher's vocation.

Although not a widely-known philosopher in the inter-national sphere, Michael Oakeshott—through his tenure of a chair in political theory at the London School of Economics—has exercised a great deal of influence on the development of political theory in England and North America. He has a number of distinguished academic followers such as Professor W. H. Greenleaf, Noel O'Sullivan and Kenneth Minogue.

Chief amongst these followers is David Manning, who has developed his own account of ideology based upon Oakeshott's philosophy. This account he presents most trenchantly in his short book *Liberalism*.

MANNING AND MINOGUE ON IDEOLOGY

In keeping with Oakeshott's philosophy, the contrast on which Manning's view of ideology depends is the contrast between academic understanding and *practical* understanding. In a way, Manning makes a commonsense complaint about *ideology* in the sense of a *political doctrine*. In Manning's view, an ideology which is a political doctrine cannot be used to attain objective comprehension of a certain state of affairs. Active involvement in society precludes such an objective assessment. The pursuit of truth is furthest from the active politician's mind.

But Manning is not simply making a point about political involvement, it is also a point about any kind of practical involvement. Following Oakeshott, Manning argues that practical involvement with a concern is different from taking a purely academic interest in it. There is a marked difference in moods. We can see this difference of mood (or approach) in the distinction Manning makes between an ideologist and a political philosopher.

'Unlike the ideologist,' he says, 'the political philosopher, *qua* philosopher, has nothing to prescribe other than the logic, or a criticism, of an understanding of politics over a period of time and in a particular place.'[14]

The academic avoids making judgements about what should be done, because his knowledge is not directly applicable to the question. The political philosopher analyses the concepts politicians use, but he is not a practical politician, since he has no interest in seeing whether such ideas work. The political philosopher 'lays bare the conceptual framework of an understanding of political experience'.[15] His object is to write a work which may potentially represent an exhaustive treatment of the subject.

There are radical differences between the worlds which the

practical politician and the political philosopher inhabit. The politician inhabits the world of practice which 'is never complete: it is always on-going. It can never achieve the degree of consistency which characterizes the intellectual masterpiece.'[16]

The political philosopher looks for intellectual coherence, he is seeking to construct a rounded, completed account. The practical, political world can never achieve such completion or internal coherence. Unlike Mannheim, who sees intellectuals as having dynamic, expanding visions of the world, Manning sees the end product of intellectual activity in the 'masterpiece'. And, he says controversially, 'masterpieces never require amendment'.[17] It is possible for a political philosopher to draw his system to a close whereas the ideologist can never draw political activity to a close.

In line with this distinction between ideology and political philosophy, Manning thinks that ideologists and academics operate with radically different conceptions of truth. An academic operates with a formal criterion of truth which establishes whether what he says is permissible or not. In the writing of history, for instance, everything is subordinated to the object of establishing what can be taken to have occurred, so that moral judgements are for the most part beside the point. On the other hand, in a tradition of ideological discourse, the interpretation of a past event which is permissible is the one which accords with the end in sight. What is relevant to the ideologist is not decided by a formal criterion of truth but rather by what squares with his programme of action.

But, despite this, ideologists do not simply ignore academic writings. Indeed, they are constantly in pursuit of academic legitimacy for the conclusions they draw. But this is precisely an attribute which characterizes ideological thinking for Manning. Ideologists are imbued with the desire to create intellectual masterpieces, although their practical vocation precludes them from achieving the goal. Because for Manning: 'The pursuit of theoretical understanding with a view to persuading men that a course of action is desirable introduces a bias incompatible with the search for understanding for its own sake'.[18]

In Manning's view, no matter how disinterested the ideologist seeks to be he cannot succeed in telling the truth in the objective sense to which he aspires. Pursuit of the truth in a scientific or historical sense involves a disinterestedness to which only the academically indifferent can aspire. Nevertheless the stab at objectivity is a hallmark of ideologies. In the attempt to get adherents, the appearance of objectivity and truth is important. An ideology supported by elaborate dissertations and learned tomes is more impressive than apparently under-researched alternatives; such scholarship or quasi-scholarship is vital for the movement to acquire new adherents. *Mein Kampf* was, in its pretensions at truth, as essential to the growth of German National Socialism as were its stormtroopers and brown shirts. Equally, Lenin even in his most propagandist of works stressed heavily the objective truth of the Marxist doctrine.

For Manning ideologies are part and parcel of political movements. They are vital to their success. All successful political movements must possess a thriving ideology. The style and object of ideologies can be deduced from the fact that they represent the 'collective consciousness' of movements seeking to defend, alter or destroy the existing condition of society. For this reason 'ideological arguments have more the character of a battle than a debate. Anyone can join in.'[19] When we think of an election campaign in a liberal democratic society, what we expect from the participants is not universal validity in what they say but rather a spirited defence of their cause or party.

Just like the movements they represent, ideologies cannot be said to have a single point of origin in time 'or to culminate in a single work'.[20] Ideologists are looking for adherents and converts, not for a dispassionate and balanced hearing. Because an ideology is the way in which the adherents of a political movement consciously relate to one another it cannot, in the end, 'be challenged by either facts or rival theories'.[21] This means that *an ideology is defined not so much by its intellectual content as by its association with those individuals and groups who espouse it*. It is possible to distinguish 'liberal authors from the contributors to other ideological traditions on the basis of their historical reputation'.[22] Liberalism is the view of the world and understanding which

Liberals espouse, just as Marxism is the view of the world and understanding which Marxists espouse. Thus, if Marxists and Liberals wish to change the view of the world they espouse they are at perfect liberty to do so. All they are required to do is to convince other adherents to the ideology of the relevance of their contribution to the common doctrine, be it Marxist or Liberal.

At heart, for Manning, '*a political ideology is intended via action, to establish the identity of a body of persons who are thereafter to be understood to be related to each other in a peculiar way*' and 'to encourage the desired consciousness the ideologist offers an interpretation of the past, and a projection of the future, based upon a prejudicial assessment of the present'.[23] A political ideology is a practical way of trying to make sense of the world. It offers individuals a way of deciding who are their friends and who are their enemies, and so creates cohesion and solidarity by providing the individual with a sense of identity.

Manning sees it as a distinctive aspect of his theory of ideology that the ideology does the work of identifying and recruiting fellow adherents to a cause. He argues that Oakeshott's strict distinction between theory and practice may lead one to lose sight of this attribute of ideology. In an essay entitled 'The Place of Ideology in Political Life', included in *The Form of Ideology*, a book of essays written with colleagues, he argues that critics of ideology such as Oakeshott and Karl Popper may have overdone their objections to the false mixture of theory and practice to be found in ideology. Manning finds them to be wholly correct in suggesting that ideologists are misplaced in trying to bring an objective, academic coherence to the practical world. Ideologists do ask too much of the world. But, in pointing out what Manning calls this 'rationalist' fallacy, they fail to see the impact an ideology, however academically incorrect, can have in attracting adherents. Ideology is primarily 'a success as instruction in the language of commitment'.[24] An ideology provides its adherents with a common vocabulary with which to distinguish the committed from the uncommitted and the innocent from the guilty. The substance of an ideological argument may often be more important than its form. The conservative thinker may not make much academic sense when he writes or speaks of the 'rule of law', or the Marxist when he speaks or writes of the 'dictatorship of the proletariat', but both are by these means able to identify themselves for their followers and supporters. Thus Manning oversteps the limits of his own Oakeshottian framework by suggesting here that an academically couched ideological argument may have an impact (albeit undesirable) on the practical world.

An ideology provides a means of asserting your identity and common interest with another like-minded individual or group of individuals. It is a badge of identification rather than a fully coherent set of ideas. This means that in any ideological tradition there need not necessarily be one writer or group of writings that fully embodies the 'ideals' of the ideology.[25] Although it is often the case that those writing in an ideological tradition regard one individual as the founding-father of the ideology, consistency with what the founding-father wrote is not a sure hallmark of adherence to an ideology. For instance, the relation of later Marxists to Marx, or later anarchists to Proudhon, is often a matter of great controversy. Thus, an ideological tradition need not possess an intellectual consistency of its own. Although those writing in an ideological tradition might wish to regard their ideas as a consistent development of the work of a predecessor, no such actual consistency need exist. Indeed, the assertion of such consistency is as much a hallmark of the ideological tradition as its existence. Manning argues that there is no essence—as there might be to an academic argument—to an ideology. This is one of the mistaken assumptions of ideologists themselves.

Another version of the Oakeshottian account of ideology is provided by Kenneth Minogue in his recent book *Alien Powers: The Pure Theory of Ideology*. Like Manning, Minogue believes that there is a stark contrast between academic and ideological activity. 'Ideologies', Minogue claims, 'neither fit, nor aspire to fit, the academic world.'[26] Ideologists in Minogue's view, are unable to come to terms with the inconveniences and imperfections of the practical world. They fail to recognize the evil inherent in human nature. Indeed if ideology were to achieve its goals the practical world would disappear. 'For practice is a transaction in which a desiring agent distinguishes itself from the rest of the world, embarks upon an activity in search of satisfaction, and thereby accepts the risk of frustration.'[27] Ideologists take a total view of experience and try to force every feature and characteristic into this framework. They ask too much of the world. They ask that individuals perfectly co-ordinate their actions with one another so that they avoid conflict. They ask that no one give in to their desires and inclinations but always act rationally and in accord with one another's needs.

To achieve this goal ideologists turn life into a battle in which there are no innocents. 'Ideology is a form of theoretical conscription: *everyone* by virtue of class, sex, race or nation, is smartly uniformed and assigned to one side or the other.'[28] Whereas the ordinary citizen might like to get on with his or her particular concerns, possibly with the individual or family context in mind, the ideologist is always out to transform the world. The world for the ideologist is a world divided into the oppressors and oppressed. And the aim of ideologists is, on the whole, to liberate the oppressed. Ideology, for Minogue, is an ailment which has particularly affected the people of the western world since about the end of the eighteenth century. Ideologists have seen the advances of western society as taking deeper and deeper steps into injustice and exploitation. 'Ideology', for Minogue, 'is the purest possible expression of European civilization's capacity for self-loathing.' Thus, although Minogue criticizes ideologists for overlooking the radical evil in man, he none the less holds that ideologists take too dark a view of our achievements. As he concludes: '. . . the most remarkable fact about ideology is its attempt to demonstrate that what by most ordinary tests—an end of hunger and the heavier burdens of labour, respect for human rights—has been a grand leap forward by mankind, is actually a monumental retardation.'[29]

In many respects the Oakeshottian view provides a conservative conception of ideology. Manning and Minogue see ideologists as out to upset the established practices of the world on the basis of wholly mistaken criteria. Ideologists fail to see that the standards which apply in practical life are not those of perfection and completion. Living a tolerable practical life requires, in the Oakeshottian view, a recognition of the refractory nature of practical problems. Such problems are not to be resolved suddenly with a new set of tools and a new set of practices. For Oakeshottians it is a question of adapting the tools which are used to ameliorate our problems and not to solve them finally. Those who believe that there are full satisfactory solutions to our practical problems are dreamers, and such visionaries should not be so rude as to impose their dreams upon others.

CRITICISMS OF THE OAKESHOTTIAN VIEW OF IDEOLOGY

A crude objection often made by students of the Oakeshottian view of ideology is that it betrays a too academic, ivory-tower approach. Oakeshottians too readily give the impression they are looking down on the affairs of the world from the insulated vantage point of the academic study. And it is indeed possible to detect a hint of intellectual superiority in the writing of Manning and Minogue. They appear to suggest that individuals involved in practical life have too little time and no great concern for thinking things through in a reasoned way. Manning appears to put an extraordinary stress on observing strictly the division of labour between mental and physical activity. In this respect Marx and Engels's strictures about the rise of the division of labour leading to the pretence that thought is something other than the thought of human individuals actively pursuing their aims would appear to apply to Manning's approach. Manning appears to believe that academic thinking is in a class apart from other forms of thought.

No doubt there is a sense in which this is true. It is a strict requirement (if not always observed) of academic thought that it follows the canons of intelligibility and rationality, and for this reason must observe the rules of logic. Whereas it is not a strict requirement in everyday life, say in a bar-room discussion or an after-tea conversation, that each participant in a discussion should be wholly consistent in what he or she puts forward. Indeed a participant in such circumstances

might fulfil a valuable personal or social function by putting
forward inconsistent claims. Whilst it is also normally expected that a contributor to an academic discussion draws a
conclusion, this is not the normal expectation of the participant in an after-tea chat or bar-room debate. What is a
permissible contribution to an academic discussion is at wide
variance with what is a permissible and expected contribution
to discussions in everyday life. So, in this respect, academic
thinking and practical thinking appear wholly distinct.

This much it is possible to concede to the Oakeshottian
approach. However, I would suggest that there is not a total
disjunction between academic and non-academic discussion.
One may find consistency in a bar-room debate just as one
may often find an academic debate, in its outward form,
indistinguishable from a bar-room brawl. Although consistency may not be a requirement of practical activity, it may
none the less bring benefits. For instance, consistency may not
be a requirement in the activity of shopping, but considerable
benefits may well accrue from consistently buying from the
cheapest source. Thus the elements that mark off academic
activity are not wholly absent from practical life, just as the
elements which mark off discussion in practical life are not
absent from academic debate.

At its most sophisticated level, this objection to Manning's
account of ideology is an objection to the Oakeshottian
idealist philosophy that underlies it. The assumption that all
experience is thinking experience—involving judgement—is
one that is difficult to accept. Some forms of experience such
as dreaming, being involved in an accident, being born and
suffering ill-health, seem to me not to involve the exercise of
judgement. Of course, reporting on such experience does
involve conceptualization and the expression of events and
occurrences in the form of ideas, but they are no substitute for
the events and occurrences themselves. The Oakeshottian
approach appears—like all idealist philosophy—to rely too
much on reflected experience and overlooks the unreflective
or passive aspect of our experience. Without the existence of
an external reality to stimulate our senses and mind there
would be no content to our thought. Once it is accepted in this
way that some of our experience may not form part of a 'world

of ideas' then the foundations for the Oakeshottian approach to ideology are undermined because the notion of an exclusive 'world of ideas' is the basis upon which Oakeshott divides our experience into separate spheres or modes.

This division seems to be the most questionable aspect of the Oakeshottian's approach. Why should philosophy, science, history and practice form distinct worlds with their own distinct criterion of truth? The connections among all four activities seem to be extremely extensive. Circumstantially, we might argue, distinguished philosophers have also been distinguished scientists (Leibniz, Aristotle), and distinguished historians have also been distinguished practitioners (Machiavelli, Marx). According to the Oakeshottian view, these individuals should have carefully isolated the one activity from the other. Yet the evidence appears to be that they saw some beneficial, direct connection among the activities. More systematically, we might criticize the way in which Oakeshott separates history from practice on the confusing grounds that history deals with the past and that practice is permanently embroiled in the future. This is only superficially a distinguishing feature of history, since no historians would claim that their activities are wholly divorced from present concerns. For instance, it would appear legitimate for historians to take into account present social structures (as many do) in trying to explain the past were they to regard those structures as more advanced forms of previous structures. As present practical concerns arise from past situations and events, the complete discontinuity Oakeshott imagines appears to be entirely artificial.

I am prepared to concede that philosophy, science and history constitute different activities, but what I find unacceptable is the suggestion that conclusions and approaches drawn from the one are irrelevant to the other. Scientific methods of research have, for instance, added considerably to the accuracy of dating procedures in historical research, just as the teaching of the history of science can help today's scientists avoid pit-falls and the errors of the past. The attempt to make these activities exclusive of one another adds an element of implausibility to Oakeshott's approach.

This is also true of the division between philosophy and

practice, which forms the basis of the Oakeshottian theory of ideology. Philosophy is defined by Oakeshott in such a way that it excludes practice and practically-oriented reflection on practice. Philosophy for Oakeshott is experience without arrest, an experience which concerns itself with contemplation upon the general nature of the world and our thought about it. Once it involves itself in practice, thinking is no longer philosophical. But it is possible to define philosophy differently. Indeed, I should argue that philosophy is more often regarded as concerned with a number of different enquiries not all distinct from practice. Logic, the theory of knowledge and ontology might plausibly be regarded as standing aloof from practical activity. However, such enquiries as the philosophy of religion, ethics and the philosophy of language cannot be regarded as external to human activity. Oakeshott tries to suggest that ethics, properly speaking, concerns itself only with the concepts of moral practice and not with the evaluation of moral practice. No doubt this is a possible way of seeing ethical enquiry, but an ethic which is neutral *vis-à-vis* the morality of actual practices is not thereby wholly detached from practice. To take a neutral stand is none the less to take a practical stand, which has implications for the world of practice.

Despite the defects of its philosophical basis, I suggest the Oakeshottian approach gives rise to some valuable insights into the nature of ideology and political ideology in particular. As Manning suggests, political ideology is a type of practical thinking which appeals on occasions to the canons of academic objectivity, but always reserves for itself the possibility of making recommendations which take no account of consistency and truth. Political ideologists are committed not to explaining what is the case, but ultimately to the survival of the ideological tradition to which they belong. Successful political ideologists identify those who share their objectives and unite them in a common cause. A political ideologist will always try to show, in Lenin's memorable phrase, 'that those who are not with us are against us'. The measure of the success of an argument for ideologists is the extent of its effectiveness in the achievement of the practical goals which flow from the ideology. For an argument to find its way into an ideology does not, therefore, always require that it be rational or true but, rather, that it should have some positive practical effect. Hence irrational contentions such as that 'all Jews are enemies of the people', or 'all Kulaks are class enemies', or 'all Communists are enemies of the Constitution', can readily form part of an ideology, although they may not withstand a moment's disinterested enquiry.

Manning and Minogue note this aspect of ideology. They see that ideologies are intended to mobilize politically and socially. To the criticism that ideologies are often misleading, they would answer that we should expect no other. Ideologies are not primarily intended to convey the truth about the world, although this is often what ideologists believe they are doing. Ideologists may aim at coherence but it is a coherence that the practical world cannot accommodate. According to the Oakeshottian view, the kind of knowledge which serves best in practical life is not the grand theory but the 'rule of thumb'. The ever-changing nature of the world makes ideologies inevitable, but it makes equally inevitable that their conceptual and moral claims can never be fully realized.

Although the Oakeshottian view is, therefore, one that is critical of ideology it is not, like Marx and Engel's view in *German Ideology*, one that is dismissive. The opaqueness that is brought to our understanding of the world through the acceptance of ideology is not, according to Manning and Minogue, one we can break through under a different arrangement of society. Some ideological claims may be academically and practically misleading, but Oakeshottians do not anticipate a practical doctrine which can avoid these pitfalls. Oakeshottians despair of bringing full perspicuity to our social relations; in some respects, they believe practical life will always remain a fog.

NOTES

1. M. Oakeshott, *Experience and its Modes*, Cambridge University Press, 1933, p.6.
2. *ibid.* p.2.
3. *ibid.* p.27.
4. *ibid.* p.331.

5.   *ibid*. p.106.
6.   *ibid*. p.193.
7.   *ibid*. p.214.
8.   *ibid*. p.81.
9.   *ibid*. p.256.
10. *ibid*. p.258.
11. *ibid*. p.304.
12. *ibid*. p.292.
13. *ibid*. p.321.
14. Manning, *Liberalism*, Dent, London, 1976, p.149.
15. *ibid*. p.149.
16. *ibid*. p.150.
17. *ibid*. p.151.
18. *ibid*. p.148.
19. *ibid*. p.11.
20. *ibid*. p.12.
21. *ibid*. p.142.
22. *ibid*. p.145.
23. *ibid*. p.154.
24. D. Manning (ed.), *The Form of Ideology*, Allen & Unwin, London, 1980, pp.88-9.
25. Manning, *op. cit.*
26. Minogue, *Alien Powers: The Pure Theory of Ideology*, Allen & Unwin, London, 1986, p.118.
27. *ibid*. p.222.
28. *ibid*. p.5.
29. *ibid*. p.221.

4 Fascism

All the principal features of a modern political ideology are combined in Fascism. Fascism offers to its adherents a complete world-view, drawn together from an immense variety of sources. Fascism is a practical doctrine that seeks to change the world; it has shown itself capable of gripping the minds of the masses; in Germany, Italy and Spain it succeeded in mobilizing a whole generation for its cause; it is anti-rationalist; and it has, so far, turned out to be both practically and intellectually wrong. More than any other political doctrine in the twentieth century, Fascism has succeeded in giving ideology a bad name.

Why was Fascism able to grip the masses so successfully in the 1920s and 30s? It seemed to do so by offering them certainty in an apparently unceasingly hostile world. The First World War and its aftermath caused an enormous dislocation in the economic and social life of western Europe. The huge casualties and the disruption of the domestic economies entirely upset the traditional balance among social classes. This chaos appeared to reflect the ineffectiveness of the old ruling groups without itself seeming to point at possible alternatives. There was a widespread belief that European civilization was heading for a fall, but no widespread agreement on the steps that should be taken to remedy the situation.

The chaos appeared to be the product of industrial society itself. Economic progress had not taken place without its costs. On the deficit side was the increasing anonymity and impersonalization of life. Side by side with the growth of industry, commerce and finance, the modern towns and cities had come into existence. Durkheim summed up, with the term *anomie*, the consequence of the process of urbanization for the individual who failed properly to adjust. He used the term to describe the feeling of helplessness and anonymity which beset the individual in the unfamiliar and hostile urban environment. As R. A. Jones puts it, for Durkheim:

In one sphere of life . . . *anomie* is not a temporary disruption but rather a chronic state. This is the sphere of trade and industry, where the traditional sources of societal regulation—religion, government, and occupational groups—have all failed to exercise moral constraints on an increasingly unregulated capitalist economy.[1]

It was this feeling which led, in his view, to one of the ills of modern civilization–suicide. In the early 1920s it could be said that it was not only isolated individuals who felt cut off and alienated from society, but whole social groups. For both the defeated and undefeated nations of Europe it appeared as though economic progress were a thing of the past; all but the very rich and powerful felt their existence threatened by inflation and unemployment. Many felt that they were living in a bankrupt society—bankrupt both economically and morally.

Fascist ideology was able to give the individual a sense of purpose and belonging in a troubled world. At a time when the state and nation were in difficulty as a result of the disasters of the First World War, Fascists were able to draw on the residual sense of loyalty to both institutions to try to reshape people's lives. They attributed the catastrophes of the war not to the nation and state themselves but to those in charge. The old ruling classes had, they suggested, betrayed the nation in its hour of need. Their corruption had led the nation to defeat and bankruptcy. Apart from the nation and the state, the Fascists put everything else in doubt. They were prepared to wipe the slate clean. Unlike all the other political parties and movements, they were wholly modernist. If necessary, they were prepared to sunder all connection with the past. This modernist programme, based as it was upon loyalty to the state and the nation, had a far more familiar and reassuring appeal than that of its great competing doctrine, Marxism. Marxists demanded an even more fundamental revision of reality than Fascism, for which a sense of history and, thus, of continuity with the past was essential. Fascism was able to mould a sense of allegiance and solidarity out of an intense desire for a sense of unity and common purpose felt by threatened social groups. In response to this desire for unity it was able to point out and, where necessary, even create powerful enemies. The greatest significance which Jewish people had for National Socialist ideology was not to be found, as Hitler surmised, in their racial characteristics but in the very fact of their difference from the German people; thus they could be made into a plausible enemy. What was of supreme importance was not that they were Jews, but that they were enemies of the German people. Fascists responded to the insecurity and instability of the modern world by attempting to make the nation-state or its race of inhabitants into the focus of all loyalty and affection. They held the existing bourgeois order in contempt and sought purity in the people and the state.

Although not a tightly-knit doctrine, Fascism evinces a number of important characteristics. I have found it useful to speak in terms of seven. Those seven characteristics are: radicalism; opposition to liberalism; support of the cult of the leader; nationalism; totalitarianism; anti-Marxism; and a tendency to glorify violence and struggle for its own sake. Needless to say, this is not intended to represent an exhaustive list of characteristics. Many others might be added and the characteristics I put forward might be subsumed under others. However, I do believe that the seven characteristics I suggest cover much of the main ground.

1. Radicalism

Fascism has to be a radical movement in order to capture the imagination of the masses. The difficulties which Fascists address in modern society—national decline, the corruption of the existing state and economic failure—seem susceptible only to radical solutions. Hitler stressed of his movement that it should not 'be an attempt to paint the shafts of the old party wagon' in different colours to suit current fashions, rather, 'an entirely new *Weltanschauung*, which was of radical significance, had to be promoted'.[2] The approach of the Fascists to politics and society was iconoclastic and eschatological. It was iconoclastic in that it was prepared to dispense with the main symbols of social solidarity of the past, be they embodied in either religion or public morality, and it was eschatological in that it intended to create a wholly new society, envisaging a new dawn in world history. Whilst preserving one or two crucial features of the cultural identity of a society, Fascists were prepared to cast away most of the rest. Everything which smacked of weakness and prevarication was dismissed with disdain and new symbols erected in their place. This rejection of the old was coupled with a millenialist commitment to the future. The Fascists saw themselves as creating a new world which would prosper for evermore, like Hitler's new thousand-year Reich.

2. Opposition to Liberalism

Fascists have no respect for the modern state as it stands. Since they are radicals, they find it at fault in a number of respects. They share with Leninists the belief that modern parliamentary democracy is a sham. At best, the representatives of the people turn up in their democratic assemblies simply to talk; at worst, they turn up to sign the attendance book so they can be paid. For Hitler, 'Scarcely anything can be more depressing than to watch this process in sober reality and to be eyewitness to this repeatedly recurring fraud'.[3] To Fascists, parliament seems more designed to resist any firm action rather than to facilitate it. On a spiritual training ground of that kind it is not possible for the bourgeois forces to develop the strength which is necessary to carry on the flight . . . against the organized might of Marxism.[4] In taking this view they are, of course, partially correct, since for liberal and conservative parliamentarians the role of the legislature is just as much to prevent undesirable measures from being taken as to carry out measures on their behalf. Since this classic view of representation (defended most strikingly by the American Founding Fathers in the *Federalist Papers*) undermines the activist role that Fascists would like to see the state playing, they object to it fiercely.

Antonio Primo de Rivera, leader of the Spanish Falange, spoke for many Fascists when he advocated a more organic form of representation than that favoured by liberals. What Primo de Rivera sought was representation through guilds and corporations.[5] This allowed a vertical integration of the state, most nearly approximated in feudal times when guild and corporation masters could for political purposes be regarded as speaking for their subordinates. Fascists found extremely objectionable the individualism to which liberalism gave rise. For them the whole should come before its parts. This 'truth' was symbolized in the corporation, where the individual attained his identity through the group. In practice, Fascists have shown their hostility to parliamentary democracy and liberal political forms by suppressing them once in power. If pressed to provide any further justification for this measure Fascists would respond by saying that Marxists, although they might be adept at employing parliamentary techniques to delay vital state policies, had no intention of observing parliamentary rules once they were in the majority. As Hitler puts it, 'Only a very credulous soul could think of binding himself to observe the rules of the game when he has to face a player for whom those rules are nothing but a mere bluff or a means of serving his own interests.'[6]

3. The Leader Principle

Fascists dismissed the liberal notion of representation on the grounds that it was divisive and too open to abuse. They took the view that what the masses required was not representation but leading. Representative politics was identified with vacillation and weak leadership. In their view, modern society was too vast and intricate a mechanism to be allowed to drift in the hands of elected leaders. Such an important decision could not be left to chance. Fascists proposed to do away with this element of chance by installing their leaders permanently in office. They suggested their leaders were better suited to the responsibilities of state because they had been tested by events and had been chosen by destiny.

At its most sophisticated this belief in the infallibility of the leader and his right to hold the destiny of his people in his hands harked back to the Hegelian idea of the great leader as the embodiment of world-spirit (*Weltgeist*). In his philosophy of history Hegel spoke of how often the transition from one important period to the next in history was marked by the emergence of a political leader of great presence and skill. Hegel thought of Julius Caesar and Napoleon as two such figures. Very often such leaders were not wholly conscious of the great significance of the move that brings them on to the stage of world history. In crossing the Rubicon, for instance, it may simply have been personal ambition or envy of Pompey that may have driven Julius on. In this, Hegel sees Julius as the unwitting agent of world spirit, who, through Julius, is advancing the course of the world. Hegel referred to such figures as 'world-historic individuals', and Fascist thinkers such as Giovanni Gentile saw Mussolini and Hitler taking on this mantle in modern times. As H. S. Harris notes, Gentile was certain with respect to Mussolini that 'the *Weltgeist* possessed him and spoke through him. In his own preferred terminology, Mussolini was simply l'Uomo, "the man" '.[7]

The idea that certain individuals were destined to rule received further intellectual support in the work of two Italian sociologists, Pareto and Mosca. In Pareto's influential *The Mind and Society* and Mosca's no less influential *The Ruling Class* it was argued that society inevitably fell into two groups, that of the leaders and that of the led. This pattern could be confirmed by even the most cursory look at history: in all recorded society it is always the minority that rules and takes advantage of its control to secure its means of subsistence from the majority.[8] This is, of course, similar to Marx and Engels's view of history. They regarded all history as a history of class struggles,[9] but Pareto and Mosca's view differs in that they see this domination in a more positive light. Pareto and Mosca wish to affirm enthusiastically inequality and élitism. Whereas Marx and Engels see a division between the privileged few and the deprived many, Pareto and Mosca see a division based on merit between the deserving and capable few and the mediocre majority.[10] Pareto and Mosca appear to note with approval the struggle of the select few to the top. Sternhell thinks that there are even overtones of Social Darwinianism in Pareto's approach, since Pareto appears to believe that the selective struggle for survival is to the ultimate benefit of society. This point of view is supported by Gregor who reports that Pareto 'as early as 1897 . . . had argued that it was an incontestable fact that men were not equal physically, intellectually or morally.'[11] Sternhell goes on to accuse Pareto and Mosca of adding to the intellectual respectability of Fascist doctrines through their advocacy of their élite theory as a universal law.

Pareto and Mosca were not the only sociologists to turn their attention to the problem of élites at the end of the nineteenth century. The famous German sociologist, Max Weber, introduced the concept of charisma in an effort to account for the apparently extraordinary hold that some leaders exercised over their followers. Weber first developed the concept in the context of the study of religions which very often centred on the life of one exceptional individual. Weber used the concept to denote the apparently magical powers that these personalities appeared to exercise over their followers.[12] The concept was then employed by analogy in an attempt to explain certain types of political authority. Weber contrasted charismatic authority with traditional authority. The charismatic leader derives authority not from any long experience of rule or connection with established power but rather from some supposed special insight and power of appeal to the people. Historically, an example of such a charismatic leader would be the Florentine priest Savonarola who governed Florence in a demagogic manner from 1494 to 1497. Savonarola came to power, after the Medicis had been overthrown by the invading French armies, through his powers of oratory, his supposed profound personal example in morality and his claim to be the mouthpiece of God. At certain disturbed times in the history of states such charismatic leaders are able to step to the fore.

The appeal of such leadership is not confined to its demagogic and revelatory powers, but is also enhanced by the opportunity it affords for the attachment to the leader of a group of trusted disciples and followers. These disciples and followers may not share the leader's magical powers but they are able to share in more mundane matters such as the fruits of office. Weber referred to his models of social behaviour as 'ideal types', intending to convey with this term that social behaviour would always approximate to the ideal type rather than realize it fully. With the ideal type of charismatic leadership it appears as though Weber's condition should be relaxed. Fascist leaders and their followers behaved as though they fully intended to realize the ideal type of charismatic leadership.

The role of the leader in Fascist doctrine is captured most strikingly by the Falange leader Antonio Primo de Rivera in a report he gives of a visit to Mussolini in Rome in 1933. Primo de Rivera says of that meeting that it did more to make him 'understand Italian Fascism than reading a great many books.'[13]

[On departing, Mussolini] returned to his desk, slowly, to resume his work in silence. It was seven o'clock in the evening. With the day's labour done, Rome was streaming through the streets in the warm evening air . . . It seemed as though only the *Duce* was still at work by the light of his lamp, in a corner of a huge empty room, watching over Italy, to whose breathing he listened from there as to that of a small daughter.[14]

Primo de Rivera paints an overpowering picture of an exceptional character, both paternalistic and visionary, whose heart-beat chimes in with the heart-beat of the nation. 'What kind of government apparatus,' Primo de Rivera concludes, 'what system of weights and scales, councils and assemblies, can possibly replace the image of the hero become father, watching beside a perpetually glimmering lamp over the toil and slumber of his people?'[15] Primo de Rivera captures perfectly the abdication of personal responsibility and freedom which lies at the heart of the acceptance of charismatic leadership.

4. Nationalism

Fascism also represents an extreme form of nationalism. For Fascists, the two immovable facts of political life are the nation and the state. Their concern is to marry the two as successfully as possible. Adherence to extreme nationalism allows them to do this.

Not all nationalism lends itself to a Fascist interpretation. The romantic nationalism of Herder, which puts stress upon each linguistic and ethnic group enjoying the freedom to give expression to its favoured customs and forms, runs counter to the exclusive stress of the nationalism favoured by Fascists.

Fascists are anxious to stress not only the individuality of their own nation but also its superiority to others. Mussolini saw Italy's claim to Abyssinia overriding any claims that Abyssinians themselves might have to govern their own country. Of this, the Fascist philosopher Gentile said:

The essential character of the spirit was only fully realized in the unrestricted activity of the nation-state; to that end the individual must be prepared to sacrifice everything—just as the ideal of nationalism led to the breakdown of empires, so the self-maintenance of the nation when it came into existence necessarily led to the creation of new empires.[16]

Hitler similarly wanted national independence for all Germans but accorded no such right to the Poles, French and Russians. With Fascists, the love of one's own country rapidly becomes transposed into a hatred of others. This xenophobic trend is not one that Herder would have encouraged. He wanted the equality of the German nation with all other nations, not its superiority over all others.

As Kedourie has stressed, nationalist doctrine is closely associated with the goal of self-determination. Kedourie associates nationalism with the moral and political thinking of Immanuel Kant.[17] The aspect of Kant's thinking which lends itself to a nationalist interpretation is his doctrine of freedom. Kant thinks an individual is free only when he can regard his conduct as regulated by laws which he himself has had a hand in formulating. Kedourie perceptively connects this notion with the doctrines of the French revolutionaries who had sought to make the nation, in the form of a representative assembly, the sole legitimate source of the law. Kedourie sees Kant as putting forward the claim that the only free person is one who is the inhabitant of a nation-state with a representative system of government. Whether or not this is an exclusively nationalist claim, it was certainly at the core of nationalist doctrine in the nineteenth century. The creation of nationally representative institutions was one of Mazzini's main demands. But this liberal form of nationalism would certainly not fall in with the Fascist model. For Fascists, their support for nationalism had little to do with the idea of self-determination. Their view was that the masses were better off without self-determination, and they loathed liberal representative institutions as breeding-grounds for disunity and individualism.

Rather than seeing the individual as connected with the nation through his exercise of electoral rights and rights of representation, Fascists preferred to see the individual connected with his nation through a bond of mystical unity. For the Spanish Falange, Spain was not 'an aggregate of men and women' it was, above all, 'an indivisible destiny'.[18] German Fascists saw the reality of the *Volk* as transcending the existence and needs of individual Germans. For the Fascist, the personality of the state takes precedence over the personality of the individual. This belief is best expressed in Gentile's mind-boggling assertion that 'the maximum liberty always coincides with the maximum force of the state'.[19]

Fascists like Gentile were opposed—in a manner reminiscent of Hegel—to the atomism of modern society. They resented the individualist and competitive nature of modern industrial society and wanted to hark back to feudal times where the individual was integrated through his job into the system of estates and, therefore, the state itself. Fascists wanted to re-create that organic connection between the individual and the state in modern society. Thus corporate rather than individual representation was integral to their nationalism. The individual's mystical bond to the state was to be cemented through his attachment to the trade, corporation or profession to which he belonged.

Sternhell argues that nationalism was particularly indispensable to Fascist leaders in the practical context because they hoped to bring together all classes of society to fight their cause.[20] The most difficult class to attract to their doctrine, but none the less the most important, was the industrial working class. Workers were the most profoundly alienated group in society, since they bore the brunt of all the huge economic dislocations. To attract their support Fascists were prepared to ascribe to socialist doctrines. Fascists depicted themselves as the opponents of the monopoly capitalists. They denounced the stock exchanges and banks for squandering the people's resources. Instead of leaving capital in private hands they sought to bring it into the control of the nation. As Mosley put it: 'Capitalism is the system by which capital uses the nation for its own purposes. Fascism is the system by which the nation uses capital for its own purposes.'[21]

The extreme nationalism of Fascists is often reinforced by a commitment to racism. The decline and corruption of the Fascist's nation is frequently connected with too great an acceptance of foreigners and individuals from another stock into the society. Fascists are often susceptible to a zoological view of mankind which sees the human race divided into various types exhibiting distinct characteristics. Since Plato's time such eugenic theories have always had a following.[22] They found their most enthusiastic advocate in Adolf Hitler. Hitler took it that the pattern of natural development was a selective one. Following the Darwinian fashion of his time, he saw the progress of the human race coming about through a competitive struggle for survival. The stronger, he says, 'must dominate and not mate with the weaker' as this 'would signify the sacrifice of its own higher nature'.[23] The great accomplishments of civilization could be attributed to the mastery of one racial group over others. It was idle and Utopian to think that this process might be changed. To spur the human species on to greater achievements, the object should be to accentuate rather than diminish the differences among races. And of course the hero in this great drama of civilization was, for Hitler, the Aryan race. But this 'greatness of the Aryan is not based on his intellectual powers; but rather on his willingness to devote all his faculties to the service of the community'.[24] Hitler contrasted this 'idealism' of the Aryan individual with the 'materialism' of the Jewish people. Instead of contributing to the state to which they belonged, the Jews were parasitical money-grubbers living off the hard work and industry of the rest. The contrast between the romantic nationalism of the eighteenth and nineteenth centuries and the racist nationalism of Hitler's Fascism could not have been more sharply brought out than when Hitler denounced the Jews for having learned German, thereby hoping to pass themselves off as good Germans. Hitler consoles himself with the thought that 'it is not however by the tie of language, but exclusively by the tie of blood that the members of a race are bound together'.[25] Herder's cultural nationalism becomes transformed into a mystic, genealogical nationalism.

5. Totalitarianism

Under Fascism, in Kogan's words, 'all aspects of human life are subject to the intervention of the state which reserves the right to provide final judgements, both value judgements and practical judgements, in all the various areas of human expression'.[26] The unequivocal answer which Fascists give to the problem of the disunity of society in its liberal phase is that society as a whole should be made subordinate to the state.

Classical liberal doctrine, of which John Stuart Mill's essay *On Liberty* is representative, distinguished between a private sphere in which the individual was sovereign and a public sphere in which the state was free to interfere. Mill contrasted self-regarding behaviour, which affected only the interests of the individual concerned, with what he called other-regarding behaviour, which was likely to impinge on the interests of others. Mill would allow no state interference in the first area, but felt that state interference was acceptable in the second area where the interests of others required protection. What an individual chose to do in his own time, with his own life and what beliefs he chose to ascribe to, were wholly private matters. Fascists could not accept this liberal dichotomy between the private and the public. For Fascists everything was potentially of public concern. The mores that people followed could not be left to chance and individual conscience. This rejection of the private sphere led to the totalitarian view of the state.

For the liberal the role of the state is limited. It serves no purpose in itself. The state exists as a convenience to ensure that the conflicts which arise from the inevitable clash of individual interests in society are regulated and resolved. Liberals of a highly individualist kind think the state should play only the role of the 'nightwatchman', providing security and upholding the law on behalf of all citizens. From the Fascist perspective this denigrates the state and detracts from its purpose. Fascists followed Hegel in believing the state was the embodiment of the ethical life of the community. In his *Philosophy of Right* Hegel speaks of the state as the realization of the ethical idea. He gives higher priority to the ethics of the community, which he terms *Sittlichkeit*, than he does to individual conscience governed by morality. Fascist thinkers,

often directly influenced by Hegel, adopted this view enthusiastically and pushed further than Hegel in seeking wholly to
subordinate the private sphere to the state. Primo de Rivera is
representative of such thinking when he proclaims that 'all the
aims of the new state could be summed up in a single word:
unity. . . . Nothing that goes against this precious and trans-
cendental unity can be accepted as being good, be those who
favour it many or few.'[27]

A strong strain of idealism was to be found in many of the
Fascists' devotion to the state. Fascists were deeply concerned
about the alienation and lack of solidarity evident in modern
society. Many Fascist thinkers were prepared to accept
Marx's account of the alienated condition of the working
class. Antonio Primo de Rivera readily granted, for instance,
that the rise of socialism was an inevitable outcome of the
harsh and uneven development of the capitalist economy.
'The workers', he said, 'had no choice but to defend themselves against that system which offered them only the
promise of rights, but did nothing to provide them with an
equitable life.'[28]

Primo de Rivera saw the modern economic system as a
system of slavery. Wage labour allowed the worker to be free
only in theory, in practice he or she was totally dependent.
The worker was legally in a position to enter into contracts of
employment and to dissolve them at will. In truth, however,
the employers were always the masters. 'Being rich,' the
capitalists are always able to say, 'we offer you whatever
conditions we please.'[29] The alternative to accepting the
employer's conditions for the worker is to face poverty and
possible starvation. The paradox of slums in one quarter of
the city and luxury in another quarter (often in close proxi-
mity) is attributed by Primo de Rivera to the two-edged
character of the labour contract.

Although they accept the socialist analysis of the conditions
of capitalist society, Fascists like Primo de Rivera do not
accept the remedies proposed by socialists. They find socialists greatly at fault for encouraging class struggle. Instead of
aiming at the greater integration of all classes in society they
see socialists as aiming for their greater opposition. Encouraging the class struggle puts sectional interest before the

interest of the nation as a whole. Fascists also deplore the materialist emphasis of socialist thinking. They see themselves as idealists and take the view that it is the excessive stress on material values that has driven society to its present state of crisis. For Hitler the most striking contrast between the Aryan and the Jewish race was that between the egotism of the latter and the idealism of the former. Jews knew nothing of the principle which most animated the German people, namely the principle of *Pflichterfullung*—the desire to fulfil one's duty.[30] As Hitler's remarks make clear, the price to be paid for the Fascist's conscientious devotion to their own nation is a complete abhorrence of any non-integrated and deviant groups within the society. This was one hallmark of the totalitarian view.

To liberal ears the term totalitarianism has entirely negative connotations. Karl Popper, J. L. Talmon and Hannah Arendt have, in celebrated works,[31] rightly denounced the belief in an all-embracing social doctrine and practice which brooks no opposition and criticism. However noble a cause (and despite the preceptions of many Fascists theirs is not a noble cause), whatever good may be achieved by advancing it in totalitarian ways will be undone by the intolerant means employed. But not all political theorists have seen totalitarianism in this way. The Italian Marxist Antonio Gramsci, who languished for much of his later life in a Fascist prison, saw merit in the totalitarian approach since it tackled the ills of modern society in what he thought to be the only practical way.[32]

Gramsci took the view that liberal society was itself totalitarian in that its beneficiaries and supporters enjoyed a hegemony over the positions of power and influence in the society. For socialists to succeed it was necessary that they adopt similar tactics. They should seek to achieve a hegemony in society, but such a hegemony could not be brought into being through force alone. Socialists should take a leaf from the liberals' book and see that the liberal influence over society was attained as much through consent as force. To attain that consent, socialists should engage fully in the cultural and intellectual battle of ideas. Nothing of note could be achieved without first of all creating a favourable intellectual and cultural climate. In Gramsci's view, Fascism in Italy owed its success to the favourable intellectual climate created by the Right in the early years of the century and in the immediate post-war period. Fascists took advantage of both modernist and reactionary trends in the culture and art of their age and understood more rapidly than their socialist counterparts the need to provide a comprehensive and colourful world-view accessible to all classes in society. In the totalitarian dimension of their thinking, Fascists grasped the deep desire of individuals to bring to an end social disunity and their grave disillusionment with all political parties. Like the Communists, they were able to exploit the desire of the politically innocent to see a total solution to the problems of social life. Fascists might all join Antonio Primo de Rivera in saying:

Down with the Cortes (the Spanish parliament) and shady politicking. Down with the Left and the Right. Down with capitalist selfishness and proletarian indiscipline. It is high time for a strong, united and determined Spain to regain control of her own destiny.[33]

6. Anti-Marxism

Fascism did not arise in a vacuum. Its rise took place coincidentally with a number of momentous events; amongst the most important of these was the Revolution of October 1917 in Russia. Marxism appeared here to have scored a dazzling success through the Bolsheviks and Lenin. Lenin appeared to have proved the power of political ideology to change the course of world events. Not surprisingly, a desire to emulate his great feat gripped other politicians, not all of them, of course, Marxists. The eccentric American writer and poet Ezra Pound, who was an enthusiastic supporter of Italian Fascism, plainly saw the connection between the career of Mussolini and the events in Russia. In his book on *Jefferson and/or Mussolini*, where he attempts to make a comparison between Mussolini and the Founding Father of American democracy, he also makes frequent reference to the parallel between Mussolini's and Lenin's achievements.[34] Mussolini was taking the same charismatic approach as Lenin in making his way to power, but in a manner better suited to Italian conditions. Fascists were both greatly impressed by the Bolshevik achievement and repelled by it. They admired the drama of the October revolution, its iconoclasm, its unleashing of the new and its rejection of the old, but they feared its social egalitarianism, internationalism, atheism and its threat to private property.

In rejecting many of the principal aims of Marxism, Fascists were none the less prepared to welcome enthusiastically its militant methods. Fascists successfully adopted the same activist style of politics as revolutionary Marxists, allowing them to compete in a most dramatic and effective way in the political market-place. There was not an act in the Bolshevik repertoire of political action they were not prepared to repeat to bring attention to themselves. Fascists called mass meetings, indeed they organized them on a scale never dreamed of by Lenin and his followers; Fascists took part in street demonstrations and marches; they engaged in picketing outside factories and public meeting-places; they distributed propaganda, fly-posted, drew graffiti; finally, like the Bolsheviks they were prepared to take power by force, thus, if necessary, to organize an insurrection.

Hitler was particularly conscious of the anti-Marxist complexion of Fascism. He saw his new national socialist party as representing the appearance of a new force 'among the timid and feckless bourgeoisie'. This force was destined to impede the triumphant advance of the Marxists and bring the *Chariot of Fate* to a standstill just as it seemed about to reach its goal.[35] He saw as the main strength of his own idea of the German *Volk* that it provided a powerful counter-attraction to the Marxist idea of an international brotherhood of man:

Only when the international idea, politically organized by Marxism is confronted by the *Volk* idea, equally well organized in a sytematic way and equally well led—only then will the fighting energy in the one camp be able to meet that of the other on an equal footing.[36]

Fascists, like Hitler, look upon Marxism as a cancerous disease spreading from the East. They were quite prepared to steal the revolutionary clothes of the Marxist leaders to ward off this terminal disease.

The notion that Fascism is essentially anti-Marxist has been most fully advanced by Ernest Nolte in his *Three Faces of Fascism*. For Nolte:

Fascism is anti-Marxism which seeks to destroy the enemy by the evolve-
ment of a radically opposed and yet related ideology and by the use of
identical and yet typically modified methods, always, however, within the
unyielding framework of national self-assertion and autonomy.[37]

Nolte's approach is appropriately dialectical. He sees
Fascism and Communism as opposites which are at the same
time united. Fascism defines itself in relation to Communism
or, as he puts it, 'without Marxism there is no Fascism'.[38]
Doubtless, this is true, but it is important to bear in mind that
Fascism was not just anti-Marxism. Fascism defined itself also
in relation to liberalism, conservatism and social democratic
thought. Without being wholly nihilistic, Fascism is the great
anti-ideology of the age.

7. The Glorification of Struggle
There is a military air about Fascist doctrine. Fascists self-
consciously see themselves as mobilizing the masses for an
impending battle. Most Fascist leaders took readily to uniform and encouraged within the ranks of their followers the
formation of paramilitary organizations. Hitler's *Sturmabteilung* (SA), Mussolini's *squadristi* and Mosley's blackshirts
readily spring to mind as examples.

These paramilitary organizations come into existence on
the basis that it is best to fight fire with fire. The Marxists were
prepared to use violence and organize an insurrection and, if
they were to be defeated, Fascists would have to employ
similar means. No one should underestimate the impact of
militarily organized groups on the development of politics.
Not only do such groups act as a magnet to attract young
people, the unemployed and the maladjusted to their ranks,
but they engender fear and the passive support of others. The
Fascist mob was a powerful recruiting organization. The dis-
located society of the post-war years of 1918-22 provided an
ideal breeding ground for the spread of such militaristic
doctrines. Many of those who fought remained without work.
Great masses of former soldiers yearned for the return of a
wartime condition in which they could regain their identity,
and military discipline might be enforced. The bases of Hitler's
Sturmabteilung and Mussolini's *Squadristi* were already to be
found in the semi-military organizations which ex-soldiers

formed, such as the *Freikorps* in Germany.

The Hungarian Marxist, Mikhaly Vajda, suggests that the resort to paramilitary organization was the most characteristic feature of the Fascist phenomenon. In his view, the party played a clearly subordinate role 'in comparison with the armed organizations such as the storm troopers'.[39] The importance that Vajda places upon the armed organizational form in Fascist politics derives from his Marxian analysis of the roots of Fascism. Vajda sees Fascism as a form of Bonapartism. We shall look more fully at the meaning of this concept in the next chapter. Vajda argues that the bourgeoisie of central and southern Europe were in an analagous position in the 1920s and 30s to that of the French bourgeoisie described by Marx in his essay *The Eighteenth Brumaire of Louis Napoleon*. They were too weak themselves to assume power and to carry out the repressive policies which were necessary to curb the ascendant and bolshevized working class. They turned instead to the semi-military organizations of the Fascists. Members of the organizations were recruited from the *déclassé* and marginalized elements of society. As Vajda puts it, 'The Fascist seizure of power meant that the bourgeoisie parted with direct political rule and handed it over to a stratum which had been driven out of the direct reproduction of bourgeois society.'[40] What made the bourgeoisie abdicate power were the 'combat troops' the Fascists had at their disposal to deal with the working-class revolutionary threat.

Primo de Rivera directly links the preparedness to use violence to the condition of society. 'Violence', he argues, 'is not systematically reprehensible, but only where it is contrary to justice. . . . Violence used against a victorious sect which spreads discord, disavows national continuity and obeys instructions from abroad' cannot be wrong.[41] As true patriots, Fascists could not be lacking in that heroism which was necessary to keep Bolshevism at bay on the streets. This preparedness to use violence at home was often reinforced by a preparedness to use violence abroad. As Harris aptly puts it in his book on Gentile's social philosophy, 'From the very beginning there was in Fascism a strain of romantic violence which was almost certain to lead to imperialist expansion in the long run.'[42] The notion of pacifism was anathema to most

Fascists. They associated the notion with cowardice, effeminacy and weakness. Those who were prepared to avoid war at all costs were not prepared to face up to the reality of international life and human life in general. Moreover, they were propounding a dull, unexciting view of human existence. For Fascists life was full of challenges which had to be faced in a manful and audacious way. For Gentile, 'The Fascist feels and affirms that life lies not in inertia, but in movement, not in the peace dear to one who is well off and therefore content to sit still, but in war.'[43] The vision is the modernist one of relentless action and conflict, where the underlying reasons for the action and conflict become of secondary significance in relation to engaging in the action and conflict. Thus Fascists idealized the psychology of the seasoned brawler and thug.

The idealization of violence and struggle was conjoined with one other fashionable doctrine of the turn of the century. Fascists were, on the whole, enthusiastic advocates of the Social Darwinian view of human progress. Hitler crudely harnessed the doctrine of natural selection to his own racist ideas. Like his precursor, Gobineau, he saw his own racist views being verified by Darwin's theories. 'If nature', he triumphantly says, 'does not wish that weaker individuals should mate with the stronger, she wishes even less that a superior race should intermingle with an inferior one.'[44] Hitler glories in the arbitrariness of nature and sees it as the model to be followed in human life. Here he finds the justification for the policy of helping the weakest go to the wall, which he was later to carry out systematically. What circumstances and nature had not favoured should not be favoured either by mankind. The glorification of violence and the doctrine of Social Darwinianism are married in the most chilling way: 'He who would live must fight. He who does not wish to fight in this world, where permanent struggle is the law of life, has not the right to exist.'[45]

NOTES

1. R. A. Jones, *Emile Durkheim: An Introduction to Four Major Works*, Sage, London, 1986, p.100.
2. A. Hitler, *Mein Kampf*, tr. James Murphy, Hurst & Blackett Ltd., London, 1939, p.313.
3. *ibid*. p.315.
4. *ibid*. p.315.
5. A. Primo de Rivera, *Selected Writings*, Cape, London, 1972.
6. Murphy (tr.), *op. cit*. p.316.
7. H. S. Harris, *The Social Philosophy of Giovanni Gentile*, University of Illinois Press, Urbana, 1966, p.219.
8. G. Parry, *Political Elites*, Allen & Unwin, London, 1970, p.36.
9. *Communist Manifesto, Selected Works in One Volume*, London, 1968, p.35.
10. Z. Sternhell, 'Fascist Ideology', in *Fascism*, ed. W. Laquer, Penguin, Harmondsworth, 1979, p.344.
11. A. J. Gregor, *The Ideology of Fascism*, Collier-Macmillan, London and Free Press, New York, 1969, p.39.
12. R. Bendix, *Max Weber: An Intellectual Portrait*, Methuen, London, 1973, p.299, p.88.
13. Primo de Rivera, *Selected Writings*, p.71.
14. *ibid*. p.72.
15. *ibid*. p.72.
16. H. S. Harris, *op. cit*. p.213.
17. E. Kedourie, *Nationalism*, Hutchinson, London, 1971, pp.21-31.
18. Primo de Rivera, *op. cit*. p.58.
19. H. S. Harris, *op. cit*. p.177.
20. Sternhell, 'Fascist Ideology', *Fascism*, p.383.
21. *ibid*. p.381.
22. Plato, *The Republic*, Penguin, Harmondsworth, 1973, pp.211-18.

    Plato is taken to task for his eugenic theories by Karl Popper in his highly critical *The Open Society and its Enemies* Vol. 1, (Routledge, London, 1977), pp.51-3.

23. Murphy (tr.), *op. cit*. p.239.
24. *ibid*. p.249.
25. *ibid*. p.261.
26. S. J. Woolf, *The Nature of Fascism*, Weidenfeld & Nicolson, London, 1968, p.11.
27. Primo de Rivera, *op. cit*. p.51.
28. *ibid*. p.51.
29. *ibid*. p.51.
30. Murphy (tr.), *op. cit*. p.249.
31. K. Popper, *The Open Society and its Enemies*, 2 Vols, Routledge, London, 1977; J. L. Talmon, *The Origins of Totalitarian Democracy*, Secker & Warburg, London, 1952.

H. Arendt, *Origins of Totalitarianism*, Harcourt Brace Jovanovich, New York, 1973.

32.　J. V. Femia, *Gramsci's Political Thought*, Clarendon Press, Oxford, 1981, p.173.

33.　Primo de Rivera, *op. cit.* p.107.

34.　*Jefferson and/or Mussolini*, Liveright, New York, 1970, pp.29, 36, 39, 91, 99.

35.　Murphy (tr.), *op. cit.* p.313.

36.　*ibid.* p.322.

37.　E. Nolte, *Three Faces of Fascism*, Mentor, New American Library, New York, 1969, p.40.

38.　*ibid.* p.40.

39.　M. Vajda, *Fascism as a Mass Movement*, Allison & Busby, London. 1976, p.47.

40.　*ibid.* p.104.

41.　Primo de Rivera, *op. cit.* p.46.

42.　H. S. Harris, *op. cit.* p.213.

43.　*ibid.* p.216.

44.　Murphy (tr.), *op. cit.* p.239.

45.　Murphy (tr.). *op. cit.* p.242.

5 Fascism and the Theory of Ideology

What light do the three theories of ideology we have looked at throw upon the Fascist doctrine? Marx's account of ideology would suggest that we look at the doctrine to discover the impact on it of economic interests and circumstances. We should, in other words, try to discover within the ideological form those elements of the material basis of society which it may reflect. Mannheim's explanation of ideology would, on the other hand, imply that we look at those aspects of Fascist doctrine which were a sign of the intellectual and social currents of the time. Fascism, according to Mannheim, should be seen as reflecting the dilemmas of the age. It was the product of a society caught between the unstoppable forces of modernism and the harsh rigours of traditionalism. We might also look at the doctrine of Fascism from Mannheim's standpoint to weigh up within it those aspects that were truly ideological (i.e. incapable of adjustment to the new era) and those which were Utopian. A question which might arise from Mannheim's standpoint would be: Were there any elements in the Fascist doctrine which might help transcend the present in a progressive way? Clearly, there were elements of the doctrine which were destructive and would lead individuals away from rather than towards a condition of adjustment. Finally, from an Oakeshottian standpoint, we might look at Fascist ideology to see what attempts its theorists make at being falsely rationalistic and so, from the Oakeshottian viewpoint, wrongly trying to bridge the gap between the world of practice and the worlds of science and philosophy. From this standpoint, Fascism would appear to abound with examples of false generalizations being drawn from the incomplete and partial experience of the practical world. Oakeshottian theory would rightly teach us to expect from Fascist thinking not theoretical consistency but a call to arms.

Fascist Ideology from the Marxian Perspective

The ringing phrases adopted by Marx and Engels about ideology seem extraordinarily applicable to Fascist thinking. In the Preface to the *Contribution to the Critique of Political Economy*, of 1859, Marx's prognostications that changes in the economic basis of society, in both the forces and relations of production, lead sooner or later to changes in the ideological 'superstructure'[1] appear to be more than borne out by the catastrophic events of the inter-war period in western Europe. The collapse of the West German economy, side by side with the huge downturn in the world economy of 1929–30 appears to have placed enormous pressure on the received modes of thought of ordinary citizens and led them to contemplate ideas which were earlier regarded as too outrageous or shocking to be entertained.

In keeping with Marx's views about the economic determination of our ideas, many historians have drawn the conclusion that the enthusiasm for Fascist doctrines shown by some members of the lower middle class, or *petite-bourgeoisie*, and the *déclassé* elements in society, grew from their economically vulnerable position. Shopkeepers, small businessmen and petty officials were threatened from all sides in the economically depressed circumstances that prevailed in Europe after the First World War. The lack of demand for consumer goods was felt first of all by the shopkeeper group, and this lack of demand in its turn took its toll most sharply on the small-scale employer. The lack of resources of these groups meant that they could only ride the economic crisis for a short period of time. What savings they had were equally threatened by inflation. The gap between themselves and the upper middle class widened, whilst the distance between themselves and the better-off section of the working class in employment narrowed ominously. As a consequence, these historians argue, members of the lower middle class were easy prey for the Fascist demagogues who appeared to provide an all-embracing explanation for, and answer to, the difficulties they were experiencing. As Carsten puts it:

Fascists appealed to all social groups . . . There is no doubt, however, that certain social groups responded much more strongly to the Fascist appeal than others . . . above all, the lower middle classes or rather certain groups within them, the artisans and independent tradesmen, the small farmers, the lower grade government employees and white collar workers.[2]

Commentators taking this view, point to the hostility shown by the Fascist movement in its early period of development to big business and the bourgeois state. As we have seen, Fascists were prepared to join Marxists in denouncing the corruption of the capitalist order. The Strasser brothers, who played a prominent part in the formation of the Nazi party in Germany, were markedly anti-capitalist in their orientation, differing fundamentally from the socialists and the Communists only on the issue of nationalism. They sought to combine socialism with the pursuit of the benefit and greatness of the national state. However, the predominant view of Fascists was not favourable to the complete abolition of private property. In keeping with its lower middle class complexion, Fascism often took a romantic view of small-scale private property and sought to safeguard it. Hostility was saved for the barons of big business, who were driving out the middleman and the family enterprise. Fascist doctrine and practice particularly favoured the peasantry. Major J. S. Barnes, a Fascist sympathizer, presents a rosy picture of the Italian peasant as 'the yeast with which Fascism looks to leaven the whole of society . . . his solid virtues are the basic materials out of which Fascism seeks to form the character of new generations'.[3] These small independent farmers were the rural equivalent of the urban lower middle class threatened, on the one hand, by decline into the ranks of the agricultural labourers and, on the other, by the acquisition of their land by the large landed owner.

Hostility to big business was often accompanied by a dislike of working-class trends towards equality. Fascists strongly believed in a careful hierarchical ranking both of society and of those who belonged to their own organizations. Society for Fascists should take on the shape of a pyramid with, at its apex, not the most wealthy, the most aged nor the most venerable but, rather, those most capable and inspired to embody the interests of the people. The way up ought not to be barred to those at the lower end of the pyramid, but progress through the ranks should depend on ability and usefulness to the cause. The corporatism which many Fascists advocated tied in with the desire not to equalize society too markedly, yet at the same time to allow greater social mobility. The concentration on one leader might also plausibly be interpreted as an attempt on the part of the lower middle orders to prevent the massed ranks of the working class from exercising too great an influence on the running of society. In order to defend their standing and position in the social order from the threat of the improving workers, they were prepared to hand all power over to one individual.

But the lower middle classes were not the sole adherents of the Fascist cause. The movement recruited enthusiastic adherents from all social classes, including the working class and the big bourgeoisie. Indeed crucial in the rise to power of Hitler in Germany was his success in ultimately winning the support of a large part of German industry. And where undue emphasis by Marxists on the petty bourgeois nature of Fascist doctrine breaks down is in the face of the non-class appeal of the movement and its protagonists. Fascists consciously sought to be members of a classless movement which put the interests of the nation, the *Volk* or the State before that of sectional concerns. Fascist leaders sought to be all things to all men within this collectivity. Hitler believed he could offer to the working class what was practical in their socialism, and to big business he offered the break-up of the power of the large independent unions. And he was able for a short time to bring prosperity to both groups by large-scale spending on re-armament. Just as many workers accepted Hiter's offer of national socialism because they saw themselves and their trades unions as too weak to fight on successfully on their own, so also many members of the big bourgeoisie abdicated to Hitler through an inability to form a strong government of their own.

FASCISM AND BONAPARTISM OR CAESARISM

A number of Marxist writers have recognized the difficulties of trying to account for the success of Fascism simply on economic grounds. They acknowledge that its appeal extended far beyond the ranks of the financially threatened petty bourgeoisie. One way in which Marxist theorists have tried to explain the cross-class appeal of the doctrine and, in particular, its appeal to the better-off section of the bourgeoisie is through referring to the phenomenon of 'Bonapartism' or 'Caesarism'.

An argument along these lines is, as we have seen, employed by Mikhaly Vajda in his *Fascism as a Mass Movement*. In the historical essay *The Eighteenth Brumaire of Louis Bonaparte* Marx speaks of Bonaparte's *coup d'état* as having been preceded by the most enormous turmoil in French social, economic and political life. In June 1848 Paris had been under the control of the revolutionary working class, who had enforced radical reforms in the system of government and election. From that period on, the bourgeoisie had sought to claw back the power it had lost. But the bourgeoisie was, according to Marx, divided amongst itself. Financial capitalists favoured one course of action, industrial capitalists favoured an opposite course, and the landed aristocracy (who hankered after the return of Bourbon rule) yet another. Whilst these divisions increased and the tensions mounted within French society, the measures which were necessary to restore order became more severe. Faced with the need to impose these extreme measures, the bourgeoisie, in Marx's view, lost its nerve. In these circumstances there arose within sections of the bourgeoisie an 'extra-parliamentary mass' which 'declared unequivocally that it longed to get rid of its own political rule in order to get rid of the troubles and dangers of ruling'.[4]

Vajda's suggestion is that a similar atmosphere prevailed in the inter-war years in Europe. The success of Bolshevism in Russia and the growing strength of the Socialist and Communist movements within states such as Italy and Germany led to a feeling of impotence amongst the ruling capitalist classes. This impotence was heightened by the severe economic dislocation which such countries were suffering as the result of uncontrolled inflation and unprecedented levels of unemployment. Just as in France in 1851, from the bourgeois standpoint the longer the crisis lasted the more severe would the measures of repression have to be. The situation became too ugly for the established bourgeois parties to handle. As Vajda puts it, 'There are cases where the bourgeoisie willingly surrenders the direct exercise of political power to other strata, and sometimes even to those who assert only the egoistic and material interests of the bourgeoisie, while considerably curtailing its rights.'[5] The bourgeoisie turned in their fear to a party and movement which had been weaned on, and prided itself on, its skill in the politics of the street. Fascist leaders made it clear both in their words and their deeds that they would not baulk from taking the most extreme measures to restore order, remove the Bolshevik threat and rekindle national pride.

Gramsci's explanation of the bourgeoisie's resort to Fascist rule is even simpler. He uses the term 'Caesarism' for the Fascist measures of self-preservation employed by bourgeois society. The Caesarist phenomenon occurs when dominant and opposed forces in society, each bent upon mastery over the other, are in a position of equal strength. When such a position of precise, 'catastrophic' balance is reached 'the conflict can only terminate in their reciprocal destruction'.[6] In such a position of terrifying balance, the opportunity arises for a third force to intervene and subjugate the warring parties. The Fascist movement and its leaders appeared to have the virtue of·belonging neither to the working class left nor the capitalist and aristocratic right. The situation was ripe for the inspired leader to pose as the saviour of the nation. The very strength of the proletariat in its momentous struggle with the ruling capitalist class paved the way for its downfall. For Gramsci the phenomenon of Caesarism need not always tend towards reactionary consequences. Depending on the quality of the heroic leader and the balance of forces in society, a period of Caesarist rule might lead to progressive change. But under Fascism the balance of forces was very much against the working class. Extraordinary Caesarist politics could only lead to its suppression.

The Marxist view is that the most favoured form of bourgeois rule is that of parliamentary democracy. Where the bourgeoisie is particularly confident of its powers it will create for itself a republic (as in the United States). Marxists argue that the capitalist class would ideally prefer such a republican form of government because it allows the class to exercise its domination powerfully and indirectly.[7] Parliamentary rule allows the great diversity of capitalist interests to be expressed, votes can be bought, congressional support can be lobbied for a cause and parliamentary advisors can direct business influence into the corridors of power. Under a democratic republic the bourgeoisie rules, but appears not to rule. Most extraordinary forces have therefore to be unleashed, according to the Marxist view, for the bourgeoisie to be prepared to give up this, its most favoured, form of rule. But Marxists, such as Vajda, argue that the bourgeoisie is always in principle prepared to abandon parliamentary democracy to survive as a class. The Bonapartists and the Fascists, according to this view, enter through already opened doors.

Another facet of the Bonapartist form of rule, as understood by Marxists, lends itself to the explanation of Fascism. In taking supreme power in France, in 1851, Louis Bonaparte was able to invoke the great military exploits of his great-uncle, Napoleon the First. According to Marx, this dash of militarism added greatly to his appeal to the French nation. Where the power of conventional politics fails, the power of the sword takes its place in all its naked vulgarity. 'The culminating point of the *idées napoléoniennes* is', Marx says, 'the preponderance of the army.'[8] The uneducated mass of the French people, in particular the peasantry, were able to identify themselves with the pomp and splendour of military rule. To the politics of disorder they were prepared to provide the most direct answer: the politics of military repression. Not used to playing the role of citizen, the rabble was able to adapt rapidly to the role of recruit. Fascism shares with Bonapartism the desire for the militarization of society. Leon Trotsky noted how:

The banner of National Socialism was raised by upstarts from the lower and middle commanding ranks of the old army. Decorated with medals for distinguished service, commissioned and non-commissioned officers could not believe that their heroism and sufferings had not only come to nothing for the Fatherland but also gave them no special claims to gratitude.[9]

The sentimental longing for a lost past under a successful military leader appears to fuel the flames of both Bonapartism and Fascism.

All Marxists accept that Fascism is the most perfidious doctrine. They associate it, almost without exception, with the final stages of capitalist society. Fascist politics they see as representing the death throes of an outmoded form of economic and social organization. This is what led to the catastrophic policy of the third Communist International, which advocated that the Communist parties of Europe work separately from the Social Democrats in bringing about the inevitable downfall of Fascism. Indeed, under the advice of Moscow, European Communists went so far as to denounce the Social Democrats as social Fascists. But this is too general a complaint to raise against the system and the doctrine. On the one hand, most analysts would agree that the triumph of Fascism is evidence of an extraordinary upheaval in society and, on the other hand, the assertion that Fascism is capitalism in its death throes is so vague as to be untestable. Does the survival of the capitalist system in Italy after the Fascist era indicate the assertion is incorrect? Adherents of the Marxist view would simply reply that the resurgence of capitalism in Italy after the Second World War represents not a cure but merely a remission of the terminal cancer. This is a colourful and (from the Marxist point of view) optimistic view of looking on the Fascist phenomenon but it can hardly be said to get at the roots of the problem.

Fascism and Mannheim's theory of ideology
As a pathology (science of a disease) of ideas Mannheim's approach is perhaps better suited to the explanation of the phenomenon of Fascism. With his stress on the need for adjustment to the requirements of the modern age and the conscious parallel Mannheim draws between his own work and that of the psychoanalyst, it would seem that he was well placed to explain the apparent mass neurosis which led to Fascism.

Mannheim sees the growth of Fascism as a part of a wider picture of the growth of social dislocation in the modern world. He shares Durkheim's view that urbanization, industrialization and the growth of the division of labour has led to a sense of estrangement or 'anomie' amongst sections of the population. Mannheim takes a long-term view of the growth of this phenomenon: 'Most symptoms of maladjustment in society can', he says, 'be traced to the fact that a parochial world of small groups expanded into a Great society in a comparatively short time.'[10] A large proportion of the members of society live in a disintegrating world. The traditional, seasonal rhythms of agricultural life are being replaced by the man-made mechanistic rhythms of factory and office life. The causes of this disintegration are not too far to be seen. 'Mere numerical increase of modern societies is a fundamental cause of our difficulties.'[11] Modern society is inescapably a mass society. Mannheim's suggestion is that mankind has found it easier to cope with the problems of production this involves, which require an improvement in industrial and agricultural technique, than it has to cope with the problems of communication and socialization mass society brings in its train. These problems tend only to be solved in a piecemeal and ineffective way.

The increase in the size of society leads, in Mannheim's view, to the increased concentration of power in the hands of a small number of individuals. This centralization and concentration of power occurs in all spheres: in industry, commerce, political life and education. The conclusion which Mannheim draws from this is that greater social planning is unavoidable. But this is not the conclusion that political leaders draw. They see only their increased power and not the underlying problems which have brought about the increase. The secularization of society leads to a cult of power but this 'exclusive emphasis on power, the neurotic complex of an age . . . destroys the world's equilibrium just as it upsets our whole mental balance'.[12] Each citizen becomes used to the greater exercise of power in the sphere to which he belongs, authoritarianism lurks under the surface in the ordering of even the most innocent of activities. This leads to a most dangerous state of affairs, according to Mannheim, since the 'raw material for chaos is not the undisciplined barbarian but the overdisciplined factory worker or soldier who as a consequence loses vitality whenever the plant closes down or where there is no one to give commands'.[13]

Combined with the growth in the means of communication, there has been an inordinate growth in the possibilities of abusing them. 'The modern shrewd technician of influence can reach the individual, as employer, as consumer, student, radio listener, sportsman or holiday maker in days of health or sickness.'[14] The improvement in the means of disseminating ideas should be of great educational and cultural benefit. The cheapness of newsprint, the availability of news on an hourly basis, and the intrusion of broadcasting into every facet of life opens up the possibility of an intelligent, well-informed citizenship. But these developments occur in an unplanned way in modern society and so are open to abuse from the unscrupulous and greedy, anxious to create a market for any fad, fashion or activity. As traditional institutions are undermined, it is not only structures and forms that disintegrate but personalities as well. Our personalities are moulded by the institutions within which we work: when they fail to remain secure our personalities are equally threatened. This phenomenon was greatly in evidence in the growth of Fascism. As businesses collapsed all around them and public services became impossible to finance, a general neurosis—bordering on panic—spread throughout the society. Intelligent citizens became vulnerable to the appeals of the first quack who believed he had the answer to the problems of the day.

The latent perplexity and moral insecurity of the little man came to the fore, and whole nations answered with the desperate cry for 'security'—the demand for something to hold on to. People considered anybody who promised anything resembling security a prophet, a saviour, and a leader whom they would follow blindly rather than remain in a state of utter instability and lawlessness.[15]

Mannheim speaks with the power and conviction of an individual who personally suffered the ravages of Fascism. Fascism to Mannheim was part of the cancer of the modern age. At the root of the cancer was the failure to live up to the necessity to institute democratic forms of planning. Planning of one kind or the other was, in Mannheim's view, totally unavoidable. In the absence of democratic planning, totalitarian planning would take the stage. Fascism was the right-wing version of this totalitarian planning, just as Russian Communism represented its left-wing version.

The dislocation of modern society was given greater force by the decline of religion. Mannheim does not restrict the meaning of religion to the practice of orthodox Christianity. Religion for Mannheim (following Durkheim and Rousseau) can take on a civic form. Religion can also be an ethic of citizenship. The most important role that religion plays from this perspective is that of integrating the life of the community. A church, chapel or civic ethic can provide a common focus of loyalty beyond individual and family self-interest. *Laissez-faire* thinking when taken too far becomes a corrosive influence and, without the influence of religion to counteract it, threatens the health of the society. There are two forces that can bind a society together—conscience or coercion. The decline of religion weakens the hold of conscience, with the consequence that greater reliance has to be placed on coercion. The stage is set for Fascism. 'While others rack their brains for ways to improve the living standard of all classes and nations, the Fascist believes only in exploitation.'[16] Fascism is the symptom of a society that has failed to recognize and deal with its own problems. Far from being a Utopia, it represents the most reactionary of ideologies:

Fascism does not believe in the perfectibility of man and has no real Utopian vision of bettering social organization and human relations. Therefore in their actions the Fascists are never guided by the idea of basic improvement of world affairs. This leads them to reckless exploitation of the immediate chances to benefit a minority, either their ruling class or their race.'[17]

Fascist ideology and the Oakeshottian theory
At the heart of the Oakeshottian critique of Fascist ideology is the view that not all are suited by disposition and ability to govern. Oakeshott and his followers believe that government is best carried out by those traditionally suited by custom, habit and practice to do the job. They are aware that this is a deeply conservative doctrine. Inspiration is drawn from Edmund Burke's attack on the enthusiasts for the French

Revolution. In *Reflections on the French Revolution* Burke attacked the view that the leaders of society may be drawn from any walk of life, provided they show sufficient ability.[18] Ability is not, in Burke's view, sufficient. Consideration should also be given to the traditional institutions of a country and its property relations. To maintain a proper harmony, traditional institutions such as the Church, the monarchy and the House of Lords should play a prominent role in the governing of British society. Oakeshottians do not see Burke as simply defending the power of vested interest in saying this. In their view Burke demonstrates a profound insight into the nature of politics in arguing that what has been in the past should govern what should be in the future. In failing to observe this rule Fascism became the monstrous doctrine that it is.

The profound insight that underlies Burke's defence of traditional forms is, according to Oakeshott, the realization that the effective maintenance and government of a society requires a distinct kind of practical knowledge. This distinct kind of practical knowledge cannot be acquired through formal education, through the reading of manuals or the teaching of others. This practical knowledge can only be acquired through the activity of government itself. This kind of knowledge, as Oakeshott puts it, 'exists only in use, is not reflective and (unlike technique) cannot be formulated in rules'.[19]

Oakeshott tries to make his point more forcibly by drawing an analogy with painting. In painting there is a great deal that can be learned through imbibing technique and observing formal rules, but none of this can of itself create the proficient painter. There is another indefinable element, Oakeshott suggests, required to create the proficient practitioner of an art. No manual of medicine will ever teach the doctor how to adopt the right 'bed-side manner'.[20] The right 'bed-side manner' can only be transmitted from the skilled practitioner to his apprentice. And the skilled practitioner will be more successful in carrying out his teaching task if he is drawing on the right material. Those born and brought up within the circles of the relevant practice are the most likely to succeed in the task of receiving the traditional skills. In general, Oakeshott rules out the young from playing the desired part in politics. He does so on the grounds that 'everybody's young days are a dream, a delightful insanity, a sweet solipsism' when the 'allure of violent emotions is irresistible'.[21] However, the Younger Pitt, drawn from the right circles was 'born old . . . and eligible to engage in politics almost in [his] cradle'.[22]

For the Oakeshottian, therefore, there are strict rules of eligibility for engaging in the practical art of politics. It is not an art for the man in the street to take up at a moment's notice. The art of politics should be carried out in a calm and considered manner, drawing on the collective experience of the traditional élites. To invite everyone to apply for the role of political leadership is to open the floodgates to, at best, mediocrity and, at worst, catastrophe.

Thus, the defect that lies at the heart of Fascist doctrine is one that is, for Oakeshottians, shared by a vast number of popular political doctrines. That political doctrines strive to be popular is itself a defect. The Oakeshottian would readily echo Hegel's view that the question of the right political doctrines is 'precisely what is not popular'.[23] Oakeshottians see the best form of government as a kind of 'charmed circle' which allows candidates to enter into its midst only after severe scrutiny and the longest possible practical apprenticeship.

Thus, in Fascist doctrine we find exacerbated, according to the Oakeshottians, one of the worst trends of modern politics. They think the process which leads to Fascism is set in train by the Enlightenment doctrines of the eighteenth century, and their practical culmination in that watershed event of the modern era—the French Revolution. According to Noel O'Sullivan, a student of Oakeshott who has written a stimulating book on the topic of *Fascism*, 'Fascism is only one manifestation of a revolutionary new style of politics.'[24] This new style of politics O'Sullivan calls 'activist'. O'Sullivan detects strains of this activism in the millenialist movements of the middle ages and early modern times, but it is in the events of the French Revolution and its aftermath that activism truly comes into its own.

The activist enthusiasm for the widest possible participation in politics O'Sullivan contrasts with what he regards as the more appropriate 'limited style of politics'. O'Sullivan, in true Oakeshottian mood, is conscious that this limited style is no longer to the taste of the age, but he laments its passing, and concludes that nothing but ill can come of disregarding its merits. Like Machiavelli, O'Sullivan argues for the autonomy of politics.

In other words, the pursuit of political objectives should not be confused with the pursuit of moral objectives. Politics deals with man as an imperfect, limited being and it leaves to one side questions of private fulfilment and moral betterment. It is the art of the possible, not the pursuit of the ideal. Because it deals with individuals as they are, as limited, and capable always of evil, true politics places great trust on the rule of law, the observance of constitutional habits and customs, and pays attention always to the national and cultural context in which political obedience is sought.

Following Machiavelli, Oakeshottians regard the state as an instrument to be used in the last resort when the normal, law-abiding relationships among individuals break down. Oakeshottians do not regard the state as capable of carrying out great tasks of moral improvement; as its basis is power, its functions under normal circumstances should be restricted. But Fascists break all the rules that constitute the core of the limited style of politics and this, for O'Sullivan, is what explains its deficiencies and errors. Once the rubric of the limited style of politics is overthrown, anything is possible. Fascists simply took to a logical conclusion a de-humanizing trend in politics which had been set in train by the Enlightenment.

There are four major features of the activist style of politics which, in O'Sullivan's view, mark it off from the limited style of politics he favours.[25] These four features are: firstly, a new theory of evil which saw evil not as arising within individuals but as being a product of social circumstances; secondly, a theory of popular sovereignty which drew its inspiration from the events of the French Revolution; thirdly, a new view of freedom which saw freedom as best being realized through a process of opposition and struggle; fourthly, an exaggerated view of the potency of the human will, a view which was again first given credence by the events of the French Revolution and its aftermath.

Activist politics bred on these four characteristics. This style of politics, according to O'Sullivan, had to go through a long process of fermentation before reaching its high point in the totalitarian doctrines of the twentieth century. Rousseau is, it seems, the political theorist who has most to answer for in this development. In his *Discourse on Inequality* he sought to contradict the conclusions of over two thousand years of human reflection when he argued that human beings were innately innocent creatures.[26] The idea that our behaviour and our morality is shaped wholly by our circumstances and education lets the individual, in O'Sullivan's view, too lightly off the hook. The misguided notion arises that if the society and its forms of education can be reshaped, the individual will be rid of the temptation to commit evil. Instead of politics being the healthy accommodation of interests it suddenly begins to be seen 'in terms of black and white' and becomes 'a matter of ensuring the triumph of light over darkness'.[27] But this is too great an accusation to lay at the door of Rousseau and the theory of the social origin of evil. O'Sullivan is in danger of lapsing into a theory of evil which is as all-encompassing as the one he criticizes. There is a great deal to the view that radical politicians tend to over-romanticize the moral qualities of the mass; however, just as it would be misjudged to say that there is a great propensity for good in everyone, so also would it be misjudged to lapse wholly into the kind of world-weary pessimism O'Sullivan appears to recommend. The human personality may not be as plastic as the activist politician supposes but, equally, it may not be as rigid as the Oakeshottian conservative supposes.

The suggestion that the doctrine of popular sovereignty has done a great deal of damage to the people of western Europe is not one that is original to O'Sullivan. He derives it most immediately from the work of his teacher at the London School of Economics, Elie Kedourie, (a colleague also of Oakeshott). Kedourie argues, in his excellent study of *Nationalism*, that the doctrine of popular sovereignty was intermeshed from the beginning with a militant nationalism.[28] Those revolutionaries who favoured popular sovereignty called for a national assembly in which all the interests of the community might be represented. On the surface, this appears the most reasonable of demands, but Kedourie believes that within it lay the seeds of the militant nationalism of the twentieth century which subordinated everything to the objective of realizing the nation's rights. What is dangerous, according to O'Sullivan, in the uncritical assertion of national political rights, is the assumption that a people can never rule itself badly.[29] Popular control of government does not ensure that the right policies are followed. O'Sullivan is perfectly justified in pointing out that in the hands of unscrupulous leaders the belief that a people's government is *per se* a good government can lead to political disaster. Populist politics is often dangerous politics, and Fascist leaders played their full share in the populist game. However, it is a perversion of the modern doctrine of democratic sovereignty to suggest that it had implicit within it elements of the Fascist programme. Fascist leaders took over power on behalf of the people; they never advocated that the people should exercise power on their own behalf.

The third and fourth aspects of the activist style of politics— a new theory of freedom as struggle, and an inflated view of the potency of the human will—O'Sullivan also draws from Kedourie's book on nationalism. For O'Sullivan, nationalism is clearly the prototype of all activist political movements. Kedourie sees nationalist thought as drawing on the philosophy of Kant and his German idealist followers, who placed so much emphasis on the role of the will and the overcoming of the most difficult obstacles in the true exercise of self-determination. That freedom is gained through opposing adversity is a most disruptive and dangerous doctrine in the eyes of Kedourie and O'Sullivan. For the best of motives, it appeared to make legitimate the most radical opposition to the established government and the perpetration in the name of progress of violent deeds. Although Kant was not a revolutionary, Kedourie and O'Sullivan see his moral doctrines as revolutionary. It was on this intellectual nourishment that the Fascist and other major activist leaders of the twentieth century were weaned.

Here the deeply conservative nature of the Oakeshottian

account of Fascism and ideology becomes evident. O'Sullivan rejects as activist, and therefore potentially totalitarian, large-scale participatory and democratic politics. Oakeshottians take a poor view of the political potential of the mass and imply that democracy is too dangerous a doctrine for members of that mass to implement. Grave political difficulties no doubt arise from allowing people to decide for themselves how best their society might be ordered. There is nothing to prevent a people from abusing the freedom accorded to it. Yet allowing political decisions to remain exclusively in the hands of the established élite is, in itself, no guarantee that wise policies will be adopted. If the mass is not to be fully trusted, it does not follow that members of the traditional ruling classes *are* to be trusted. The evidence suggests that the traditional élites were as much to blame, possibly more, for the advent of Fascism as were the untutored, over-enthusiastic masses. Overall, the Oakeshottian school offers too complacent an approach to the problems of politics. The problem of marrying the exercise of power and political participation is continually in evidence in modern societies. There appears to be no simple, straightforward answer. It certainly ought not to be swept to one side, in the Oakeshottian manner, in a nostalgic yearning for the limited (possibly dynastic?) politics of the pre-modern era. Here Mannheim's approach shows greater realism and offers far greater hope.

The *ennui* which O'Sullivan evinces towards the mass politics of the modern era, and his contention that the disease first took hold at the time of the Englightenment, is reminiscent of the thesis advanced (from an entirely different point in the political spectrum) by Horkheimer and Adorno in their book *Dialectic of the Enlightenment*. This book, written in exile during the last war by these two members of the Neo-Marxist Frankfurt School, discovers the roots of Fascism and anti-Semitism in the enthusiastic empiricist and scientific doctrines of the Enlightenment thinkers. Thinkers such as Bacon, Locke, Gassendi and the French *philosophes* inadvertently opened the door to the domination of technology and instrumental reason over our lives. Horkheimer and Adorno 'are wholly convinced . . . that social freedom is inseparable from enlightened thought. Nevertheless we believe that we just as clearly recognized that the notion of this very way of thinking . . . contains the seed of the reversal universally apparent today.'[30] For different reasons, Horkheimer and Adorno are just as sceptical of the positive nature of enlightenment thinking as O'Sullivan. However, they do not wholly side with O'Sullivan in rejecting the optimism of the Enlightenment. With great care they believe the process of enlightenment can be saved from its worst consequences.

But in one respect there is great merit to O'Sullivan's account. Fascism can be accurately represented as a form of politics which sought to set to one side all the normal rules of constitutional government. Traditional constitutional government and Fascism are at opposite poles. A great deal can be learnt about Fascism by looking closely at this contrast. O'Sullivan, as we have seen, proposes four points of particular contrast. But the grave problem with the Oakeshottian explanation of Fascist ideology is its generality. O'Sullivan sees his theory as explaining the success of Fascism *and* Communism; more than this, he sees it as explaining the success of modern mass political movements as a whole. But such a theory, however informative it may be in its parts, is too all-exclusive to warrant being regarded as sufficient explanation of Fascism. As well as knowing what features Fascism shares with ideology as a whole, we would also expect a theory of ideology to tell us what the specific features of Fascism were and how, therefore, it was distinguished from other ideologies.

NOTES

1. K. Marx, *Contribution to the Critique of Political Economy*, Lawrence & Wishart, London, 1971, p.21.
2. F. L. Carsten, *The Rise of Fascism*, Batsford, London, 1980, pp.9-10.
3. J. S. Barnes, *Fascism*, Butterworth, London, 1931, p.70.
4. K. Marx, 'The Eighteenth Brumaire of Louis Bonaparte', *Selected Works of Marx and Engels in One Volume*, Lawrence & Wishart, London, 1968, p.160.

5. M. Vajda, *Fascism as a Mass Movement*, Allison & Busby, London, 1976, p.102.
6. A. Gramsci, *Prison Notebooks*, Lawrence & Wishart, London, 1971, p.219.
7. Cf. Lenin, *State and Revolution*, Foreign Languages Press, Peking, 1965, pp.15-16.

    A democratic republic is the best possible political shell of capitalism, and, therefore, once capital has gained control of this very best shell . . . it establishes its power so securely, so firmly, that no change, either of persons, of institutions, or of parties in the bourgeois-democratic republic, can shake it.

8. K. Marx, 'Eighteenth Brumaire', *Selected Works*, p.177.
9. L. Trotsky, *The Age of Permanent Revolution*, ed. I Deutscher, Dell, New York, 1964, p.175.
10. K. Mannheim, *Freedom, Power and Democratic Planning*, Routledge & Kegan Paul, London, 1951, p.4.
11. Mannheim, *op. cit.* p.6.
12. *ibid*. p.11.
13. *ibid*. p.14.
14. *ibid*. p.15.
15. *ibid*. p.19.
16. *ibid*. p.25.
17. *ibid*. p.25.
18. E. Burke, *Reflections on the Revolution in France*, Penguin, Harmondsworth, 1973.

    p.138: 'The occupation of an hair-dresser, or of a working tallow-chandler, cannot be a matter of honour to any person—to say nothing of a number of other more servile employments. Such descriptions of men ought not to suffer oppression from the state; but the state suffers oppression, if such as they, either individually or collectively, are permitted to rule.'
    cf. also p.140: 'Nothing is a due and adequate representation of a state, that does not represent its ability, as well as its property.'

19. M. Oakeshott, *Rationalism in Politics*, Methuen, London, 1967, p.8.
20. *ibid*. p.9.
21. *ibid*. p.195.
22. *ibid*. p.196.
23. G. W. F. Hegel, *Philosophy of Right*, Oxford University Press, 1971, para. 30, p.196.
24. N. O'Sullivan, *Fascism*, Dent, London, 1983, p.i.
25. *ibid*. p.41.
26. *ibid*. p.42.
27. *ibid*. p.42.
28. E. Kedourie, *Nationalism*, Hutchinson, London, 1971, pp.12-13.

29.   N. O'Sullivan, *op. cit.* p.48.
30.   M. Horkheimer & T. Adorno, *Dialectic of the Enlightenment*, Allen
       Lane, London, 1973, p.xii.

6 Two Contemporary Theories of Ideology

Louis Althusser's structural Marxism

Current thinking on ideology has been much dominated by the French. Aided by the hold that structuralist philosophy has over French academic thinking as a whole, a great deal of attention has been paid to the problem of ideology. As the name suggests, structuralism concerns itself with the possible uniform patterns that may underlie a situation or occurrence. For example, those structuralists that have turned their attention to language and speech have placed great stress on the underlying patterns which make possible coherent human utterances and discourse. Structuralists, in brief, always have an eye for the system of factual relations which may help to explain an event or a state of affairs.

The French Marxist philosopher Louis Althusser was an important figure on the Left in the 1970s. His work was imported enthusiastically to Britain and the United States on the wave of student radicalism of the late 60s. Althusser's star has waned somewhat now, so much so that a recent work by Ted Benton addressed to his philosophy is entitled *The Rise and Fall of Structural Marxism*.[1] None the less, Althusser has exerted an important influence upon recent thinking on ideology through his attempt to reformulate Marxism along his own personal lines.

A distinction which Althusser strongly insists upon in his account of Marxism is the distinction between science and ideology. This distinction comes to the fore in the interpretation Althusser provides of Marx's intellectual development. In Althusser's view there is a marked difference between

Marx's earlier humanistic writings (composed mainly in Paris and Brussels between 1844 and 1847) criticizing such things as alienation, poverty and religious discrimination, and Marx's later systematic writings (composed in London from 1848 onwards) analysing the nature and dynamic of capitalist society. Althusser put forward the controversial thesis that in the period 1845–6 there occurred an 'epistemological break' in Marx's intellectual development when he abandoned many of the earlier humanistic themes of his writings. It is this 'break' in Marx's view of the nature of knowledge which marks, according to Althusser, the transition to science in his writings. Thus, although Althusser is not wholly happy with *Capital* (particularly its seemingly Hegelian sections), he unequivocally accepts it as belonging to the corpus of Marx's scientific work.

What this distinction between science and ideology implies for the nature of science is not always clear. Science, it appears, is more intelligible and open than an ideology. Ideologies are also, it seems, tied to material practices (or day-to-day economic activities) whereas science forms more or less exclusively a *theoretical* practice. If we regard Marx's *Capital* as exemplifying the scientific form, we can see science, in addition, as seeking the structures which underlie the world manifested to our senses and conveyed to us in our language and ideas. Science, it appears, takes it for granted that there exist intricate connections and regularities which account for the objects and events we observe in the world. The task it sets itself is to bring to light these connections and regularities. That Althusser sees them as a structure is, of course, in keeping with his own philosophical background in French Structuralism. Science, for Althusser, seeks structural causes for the actions and events we observe in the world. Thus, as Steve Smith points out, Althusser identifies science with structuralism.[2]

Ideology takes on an entirely different form. The function of ideology is not to explain, it is to situate the subject in the world as a practically active being. For Althusser ideology is firmly tied to the conditions of production and reproduction of a society. In Marxian terms, he says, 'the reproduction of labour power requires not only a reproduction of its skills, but also, at the same time, a reproduction of its submission to the rules of the established order'.[3] This point is well put and thus far wholly falls in with the account Marx gives of ideology as something which arises from our productive activities. Because of the aura of privacy which the market casts over the production process, we are inclined to think of the continuation of the processes of production of society merely as a technical and economic matter. However, the success or otherwise of a system of production is also a social affair. The producers in a society have not only to be conversant with the tools and technical rules of production but also have to be socialized into the legal and economic forms which make possible a mode of production. No one is actually born a wage worker or employee; rather these roles have to be learned and acquired. It is in this process of acquisition and learning, according to Althusser, that ideology performs one of its main tasks.

Althusser accepts the distinction Marx makes between the society's economic base and its ideological superstructure in the Preface to the 1859 *Contribution to the Critique of Political Economy*. He takes the view, first advanced by Engels, that the metaphor is intended to suggest that the nature of the ideological superstructure is determined only 'in the last instance' and not in every detail by the economic base.[4] The formula is not, therefore, to be applied too rigidly and is most valuable when it is developed further and more fully. The analyst must recognize, for instance, that not only does the economic base act upon the superstructure, but also that the superstructure in its turn influences the base. Another precept Althusser derives from the Marxist tradition is that the realm of ideas which forms the ideological superstructure should be regarded as relatively 'autonomous'. By this Althusser means that the possibility of independent intellectual developments not wholly influenced by the economic base, and which can in their turn influence this base, should not be ruled out.

Where Althusser's theory of ideology begins to differ from Marx's account in the *German Ideology* is in the emphasis he places on the state in the maintenance and dissemination of ideology. This emphasis Althusser believes he shares with Gramsci. In Marx's day, economy and polity were less intertwined than they are now, so it was possible to see the ideological thinking of individuals developing both from their social and political contexts. A point that Gramsci grasps, writing some seventy years after Marx, is that in many instances economic and social institutions have become part of the state.

Althusser therefore endorses a modification of Marx's political theory whereby the state apparatus is no longer seen as consisting primarily of the repressive institutions (i.e. institutions that use force or the threat of force, such as the army, the police, the prison system and the courts) that the ruling class has at its disposal, but consists also of apparently neutral institutions such as the educational system, the family, the legal profession and religious institutions. Marx always recognized the influence of such institutions upon ideology, but did not, as do Gramsci and Althusser, regard them as part of the state apparatus. Althusser coins the term 'ideological state apparatuses' to refer to these institutions. For Althusser these ideological state apparatuses fall into a remarkable eight spheres: the religious sphere, the educational sphere, the family sphere, the legal sphere, the political sphere (political parties etc.), the trades unions sphere, the communications sphere and the cultural sphere. The interesting and novel inclusions within this list are the trades unions and political spheres. Their inclusion seems problematic since we are so used to regarding these spheres more as oppositional spheres than as spheres of support for the state. But Althusser would no doubt argue that such has been the advance of the power of the state and its permeation into all spheres of society that the ideological power of the state even conditions the thinking and action of such apparently oppositional groups. Indeed, one might even argue that nothing more legitimizes the power of the state than the tolerance of, and integration into, the state of powerful oppositional forces.

Where these ideological state apparatuses differ from the other repressive state apparatuses is in the extent to which they enter and take over the private domain. Through the influence the state exerts on the educational system and on the system of communications, it can enter as an equal, or even as master, the everyday lives of its citizens. As Althusser points out, so powerful has become the influence of such indirect means of exercising power that nowadays 'no class can hold state power over a long period without at the same time exercising hegemony over and in the State ideological apparatuses'.[5]

Althusser is, perhaps surprisingly, in no doubt that the 'ideological State apparatus which has been installed in the dominant position in mature capitalist social formations . . . is the educational ideological apparatus'.[6] The influence of the church and chapel on our thinking has given way to the influence of the school, college and university. The influence of such ideological state apparatuses is exerted primarily through the inculcation of certain ideas and practices, but various forms of coercion can also play a subordinate role. As well as their teaching role, educational systems also have their methods of discipline, just as a church can wield power over its members through the threat of discrimination or, ultimately, excommunication.

Althusser believes that this theory of ideological state apparatuses can be extrapolated from Marx and Marxist thinking. However, he is not prepared to attribute to Marx a properly developed theory of ideology. He acknowledges that the inability to do this is 'a rather astonishing paradox'.[7] Everything might lead us to suppose that Marx has to formulate a theory of ideology, yet in the book which carries the title *German Ideology* we do not see, according to Althusser, a theory of ideology. Here Althusser is, I think, on rather shaky ground because, as we have seen, there is a theory of ideology to be discovered in Marx's earlier writings. What is true, though, is that this is not Althusser's theory of ideology.

Althusser puts forward a number of detailed and controversial theses about the theory of ideology. The first of these theses is that 'ideology has no history'.[8] Despite the suggestion at one stage in his argument that he follows the classical Marxian view which sees ideology as a peculiar feature of a class society and would, therefore, be expected to disappear in a classless society, Althusser's *predominant* position appears to be that ideology is a timeless phenomenon necessary in any society. This impression is confirmed by Althusser's taking the view that man is an 'ideological animal' by nature. Althusser comes to this conclusion because, unlike Marx, he believes ideological thinking is always crucial to our situating ourselves in the world. Ideology for Althusser is heavily intertwined with the material practices which help constitute our world. In arguing this, Althusser does not distinguish between peculiarly capitalist economic practices and generally necessary social and economic practices. Since the organization of the division of labour remains a problem for any society, there will always, according to Althusser, need to be a set of ideas which correspond with a given division of labour. Ideology grows out of our material practices in an unavoidable way. In so arguing, Althusser sets to one side one of the principal features of Marx's critical theory of ideology.

Althusser's second thesis is that 'ideology is a "representation" of the imaginary relationship of individuals to their real conditions of existence'.[9] This is close to the classical Marxian view that ideology represents an inverted understanding of our social relationships, attributing false powers to objects and individuals. Here, as with Marx also, there is the implication that if we can come to understand our real relations we can discover the source of our ideological illusions. But, whereas Marx attributes these ideological illusions to the nature of capitalist society, the implication of Althusser's analysis is that in any society individuals will need to relate to each other in imaginary ways.

An important point this thesis of Althusser's brings out is the subjective, relational nature of his theory of ideology. Althusser argues that what is misleadingly represented in ideology is not our real relations of production themselves— since the producers in a capitalist society rarely grasp what they are anyway—but the manner in which we relate to those real relations. Ideology is a subjective thought-construct rather than an objective response to economic circumstances. It arises from the individual's need to locate himself or herself in the world. Where our perception of the relations of production are unclear and misleading, this leads to an unclear (or ideological) conception of our place in the world. Our thinking is twice distorted, first by the attempt to depict our productive relations in thought and, secondly, by the unclear nature of our perception of our productive relations. However, Althusser stresses, the imaginary nature of this account of our place in the world detracts from a point which is most important to Marx, that is, that ideological distortion in a capitalist society is necessary and unavoidable. For Marx there is an objective process that takes place here. Ideological thinking is imaginary for Marx in the sense that it fails properly to explain our circumstances. However, there is nothing imaginary about the hold it exercises over individuals: its power is as real and profound as any true set of ideas. This power derives from the present structure of our real relations of production. For Marx there is but one distortion and this arises from the nature of productive relations themselves.

Althusser's third thesis that 'ideology has a material existence'[10] appears to confirm this point. What Althusser means by this is that an individual's adherence to an ideology is most clearly seen in the habits and customs he or she observes. The key ideas of an ideology have a practical import. Althusser takes as his example the hold that religious thinking has over its adherents. Belonging to a faith not only requires an attitude of mind but also crucially requires that certain practices be observed. The good Catholic attends mass regularly, goes to confession, kneels before the altar, takes communion, prays and does penance. Without observing such practices, the individual ceases to be a Catholic.

Certain material practices therefore always flow from the acceptance of an ideology. In an inactive, contemplative state of mind only part of an ideology evinces itself in certain attitudes and dispositions. Althusser can draw on the authority of Marx in taking this view, since Marx's major concern in criticizing ideology was to reveal the distinct orientation to praxis an ideological position usually concealed. However, Althusser goes further than Marx in presenting his theory of ideology as a theory of practical activity. For Althusser an individual's 'ideas are his material actions inserted into material practices governed by material rituals which are themselves defined by the material ideological apparatus from which derive the ideas of that subject. . . . These practices are governed by the rituals in which these practices are inscribed, within the material existence of an ideological apparatus, be it only a small part of that apparatus: a small mass in a small church, a funeral, a minor match at a sports club, a school day, a political party meeting, etc.'[11] In his account of ideology Marx does not concern himself with such commonplace, humdrum examples. His major concern was with the literary and scientific distortion and misinterpretation of established facts. Ideology might, for Marx, be in evidence in such day-to-day social activities, but he sees the source of ideology as lying outside those spheres in economic production. Here, there is a closer affinity between Althusser and the Oakeshottian idealists in his practical, subjective view of ideology than there is between Althusser and Marx. This can be seen clearly in the two further theses about ideology Althusser advances: that (1) 'there is no practice except by and in ideology and [2] that there is no ideology except by the subject and for subjects'.[12].

Clearly there is a decisive break between Marx's view of ideology and Althusser's. Marx envisaged that the practice of a Communist society would do away with the need for ideology. Ideology would cease to be necessary in such a society because the productive relations of individuals to each other, as free individuals engaged in economic activity following an agreed economic plan, would be wholly clear. Investment, production and distribution would be wholly co-ordinated from the beginning, so that misconceptions about the relation of one producer to the other would cease to arise. Althusser departs from this vision by connecting ideology, in an Oakeshottian idealist fashion, with practice. Ideology takes on a different meaning from that in Marx's critical theory, when it is seen as part and parcel of any human practice. We may wish to say that the ideas we employ in co-ordinating a certain form of activity, such as organizing a political party, directing a play or planning a work of art, form an ideology, but here ideology is being used more in the sense of doctrine or world-outlook than in the specialist sense primarily envisaged by Marx.

The final, intriguing thesis put forward by Althusser—and here the debt to structuralism rather than Marx is apparent— is that 'ideology interpellates individuals as subjects'.[13] This thesis ties in with the materialist account which Althusser gives of ideology. He sees ideology arising in the process of the reproduction of the society. Society has eternally to reproduce itself, that is, it has to ensure that a large part of its members and institutions survive or are replaced from one year to the next. Ideology ensures that each individual knows his or her place in the division of labour and knows culturally how to respond to the demands made by taking that place. This thesis simply takes this view further by arguing that in locating the individual in the social order, ideology also shapes that individual's identity. A subject is a person who knows his or her (subordinate) place in the world and knows how properly to respond to the commands of the world's rulers.

This is an intriguing thesis because it takes up some important contemporary philosophical themes. One key theme in contemporary Anglo-American philosophy, developed in particular by the Oxford philosopher Derek Parfit,[14] is that personal identity exists primarily in the form of a number of social relationships. Our subjectivity is not something which merely inheres in our mental and physical being but is brought into existence and stimulated into fuller development through our relationships with others. Althusser grasps this as an ideological process. In his view, it can occur almost instantaneously, as when a policeman hails a passer-by. Through the action of hailing, the policeman transforms the individual amongst a crowd of others into a subject. No longer an innocent, indistinguishable individual amongst the mass, the hailed individual is transformed into a subject—the object of police surveillance. According to Althusser, this process occurs continuously in all walks of life and it is the process which gives us subjects with both personalities and ideology. As Althusser puts it, 'The existence of ideology and the hailing or interpellation of individuals as subjects are one and the same thing.'[15]

This is an interesting way of demonstrating how crucial others are to the creation of our subjectivity, but it is difficult to see it as a convincing account of ideology. It is possible to see how the process of 'interpellating individuals as subjects' helps transmit an ideology. For instance, we might regard the random hailing of individuals by the police in a large city as evidence of the grip of an authoritarian ideology upon a society, but it is not likely that we should like to see the normal process of street policing as in itself ideological. Should we wish to do so the category of ideology becomes so broad that it can hardly be distinguished from the less threatening-sounding conception of socialization. Most would accept the thesis that we are socialized into being what we are, or that our subjectivity is a product of our experience of others as well as ourselves, and prefer to retain the notion of ideology for an accentuation or distortion of desired or 'normal' forms of socialization.

Althusser connects the process of creating an identity through ideology with the formation of a background notion of an absolute subject. This thesis appears to derive from Althusser's analysis of religion. All the recognized forms of address in the Christian religion, such as the Ten Commandments, take for granted the existence of an absolute subject— God—who gives coherence to the modes of address and legitimizes their content. To be of the faith requires a subject to whom one can be faithful. In being faithful to the one subject, we can affirm our existence as subjects. As Althusser stresses, there can be no subjects without their being a centre-point to which they can all relate. From this recognition of the absolute subject flows our acceptance in and by the world. Through mediating our subjectivity in the absolute subject we become certain of ourselves.

Althusser seems to have hit upon an important aspect of some ideologies here. Authoritarian ideologies would seem to grow on this fertile ground of individuals wishing to be recognized as subjects in the world. Fascist ideology drew strongly on the desire for certainty and wishing to know your place in the world. However, Althusser is wrong to imply that this is an eternal condition of the formation of human societies. It is possible to conceive of societies where individuals have not conceived themselves as subjects (e.g. slaves in a slave society) and it is quite unremarkable to come across modern citizens who would wish not to be seen wholly as subjects. The republican ideal where each citizen is seen as equal is, of course, not often realized, but that the ideal has had such a firm hold, for instance on Althusser's own French society,

suggests that not all individuals always desire or necessarily
have to see themselves as subjects.

Ricoeur: taking the suspicion from ideological analysis

Paul Ricoeur draws on two themes in modern philosophy,
structuralism and phenomenology. Ricoeur shares the structuralist theme with Althusser, the phenomenological theme
he derives, however, from the philosophy of Husserl. The
principle tenet of Husserl's phenomenology was that all experience derives from appearance, that is, all that we sense
and observe in the world. A starting point for Ricoeur's
account of ideology is the Ancient Greek philosopher Aristotle's famous claim in his *Ethics* that we should seek from any
sphere of human study only that measure of authority and
certainty which the subject matter allows. Aristotle argues
that in the spheres of politics and ethics we cannot hope for
the same level of precision as in the study of nature. This claim
sheds a critical light on the distinction between ideology and
science—so crucial to Althusser's account of ideology.
Althusser, like many other social theorists and philosophers,
holds that whenever thought is ideological it cannot possibly
also be scientific. But where we admit from the beginning that
the project of creating a truly systematic science of society is
over-ambitious, or even hopeless, then the notion that some
social doctrines or commonly held ideas are totally incorrect,
or 'ideological' in Althusser's sense, seems unnecessarily
rigorous and high-minded.

For this reason Ricoeur thinks 'it is necessary . . . to loosen
the link between the theory of ideology and the strategy of
suspicion'.[16] Here Ricoeur is not only hitting at Althusser but
also Marx. Marx was deeply suspicious of ideology, although
he believed that the route to a clear understanding of society
was through a critical appreciation of ideology. But where
none of our ideas about society is regarded as unequivocally
scientific, equally none can be regarded as wholly misguided.
Whereas Marx would wish to free his thought from ideological influence, Ricoeur believes that no such separation is
possible. For Ricoeur the problem is coming to terms with our
social thinking, which is always tinged with an element of
ideology.

As with Althusser, Ricoeur sees ideology as a necessary feature of society. An ideology is what gives to a social group its collective personality. 'Ideology', Ricoeur says, 'is linked to the necessity for a social group to give itself an image of itself.'[17] What originally gives a social group its cohesion is the act which brings it to prominence and then political power. However, this crucial founding act can never be empirically repeated. The role that an ideology plays is to keep alive symbolically this founding act. Ideology, Ricoeur astutely notes, is a function of the distance that separates the social memory from 'an inaugural event which nevertheless must be repeated'.[18] The group's act of self-realization, such as that of the Founding Fathers of America, the republican revolutionaries in France and the Bolsheviks in Russia, has to be kept alive for the 'personality' and homogeneity of that group to be retained. Thus, for Ricoeur, ideology in modern society appears to play a role somewhat analagous to the role played by the foundation myth in ancient societies. It romanticizes and idealizes the past in order to retain the present cohesion of society.[19]

For Ricoeur ideology is never high theory. He would not attempt, as did Marx, to discover ideology first in political economy and philosophy. Ideology for Ricoeur is first and foremost necessary for social cohesion. There is a straightforward reason for this. For a set of ideas to become generally held they require simplification or popularization. In this process we can observe the paradox that 'thought loses its vigour in order to enhance its social efficiency'. In becoming ideology, the status of a set of ideas changes from being that of a belief into being *expressions of opinion*. The intellectual currency of everyday life cannot, in Ricoeur's view, absorb systematic theory. Intellectual systems have first to be broken down into opinions for them to gain full access to the ordinary consciousness. Ricoeur is not merely concerned with this fact from an educational point of view; since a society cannot be properly integrated unless it boasts a common currency of opinions, the higher level beliefs will not suffice. For a new theory to enter this consensus requires a process akin to that of translation—from the sophisticated language of intellectual discourse into the more concrete and illustrative forms of thought current in life. As Ricoeur astutely puts it: 'Social cohesion can be unquestionably secured only if the doxic threshold which corresponds to the average cultural level of the group concerned is not surpassed.'[20] In other words, an ideology has to employ the common vocabulary of the society if it is to succeed.

Ideology is then, from Ricoeur's standpoint, inescapable. This view he encapsulates in the claim: 'We think from it rather than about it.'[21] Ideology is the grid of ideas through which we come to know the world. There is no mind that is sufficiently comprehensive to encompass all that can be said, done and experienced in the world. We all feed off the ideologies of our time. Thus, the vast majority of our ideas are second-hand or inherited. New experiences come to us through this grid. It is only at a second level of reflection that we can become conscious of the ideology in our own thinking.

This view of ideology as pervasive and inescapable leads Ricoeur to a highly sceptical attitude towards those analysts of ideology who claim superior, non-ideological insight. In his estimation there can never be an absolute freedom from ideology in our thinking. Here, clearly, Ricoeur departs from Marx and Engels's vision of a non-ideological Communist society of the future. Any such freedom we may aspire to has always to be relative. We cannot analyse ideology from on high. We have to analyse it from within, as fellow-subjects or sufferers.

Contrary to Marx and Althusser, Ricoeur does not therefore favour a marked antithesis between ideology and science. In Ricoeur's view, the only sense of science which would sustain such an antithesis is what he calls a positivist one. The positivist thinker sees science as confining itself to the explanation of observed phenomena. The evidence of the senses is primary for the positivist. Events have to be measurable and readable to come within the purview of science. Such a view of science conforms with the techniques employed in natural science in its foundational period in the course of the Enlightenment but does not, according to Ricoeur, meet with the speculative techniques of the post-Einsteinian physics of today. Whatever the doubts there are about whether or not this positivist notion of science conforms with the practice of contemporary science, what is not in doubt is that such a positivist notion rules out the possibility of an extensive and successful social science. All social research is necessarily reflective and has to go beyond the mere observation of facts. We cannot rely solely on sense-data and observation in building up an understanding of the social world. As Ricoeur concludes, if we adhere to a positivist view of science there can be no ideology/science distinction because there can be no social science.

However, if we reject the positivist view of science as inapplicable to the human sciences, this 'entails *ipso facto* the abandonment of a purely disjunctive conception of the relation between science and ideology'.[22] In other words, we cannot see the sphere of science and the sphere of ideology as two opposed worlds. Ricoeur draws upon two important contemporary German thinkers, Gadamer and Habermas, to develop a model of human and social studies which does not rely on a break between science and ideology, and thus provides a more satisfactory theory of ideology. The hermeneutic tradition, represented by Gadamer, particularly appeals to Ricoeur. Hermeneutics developed originally as a theory of the interpretation of texts—particularly important, as one might imagine, in philosophy and theology. However, the hermeneutic technique was gradually given a wider use, and in the philosophy of Wilhelm Dilthey became the basis for a general account of experience. Hermeneutic philosophers, such as Dilthey and Gadamer, place a strong emphasis on the importance of *tradition* in the formation of our experience. We come to think within a historically circumscribed environment. For Gadamer prejudice precedes judgement. Prejudice has a pejorative connotation nowadays but for the hermeneutic philosopher there is, as there was for Burke, a merit in prejudice positively understood as a predeliction towards a certain outlook—one which conformed with tradition. As Gadamer puts it:

The overcoming of all prejudices, this global demand of the Enlightenment, will prove to be itself a prejudice, the removal of which opens the way for an appropriate understanding of our finitude, which dominates not only our humanity, but also our historical consciousness.[23]

Ricoeur draws on Habermas's view that all knowledge is interest-related to develop a conception of the critique of ideology which is tolerant of the diversity and heterogeneity of human experience. Habermas's approach is not, however, tolerant to the extent that it acknowledges (as does that of Gadamer) traditions as they stand. Habermas defends a notion of a superior interest-related form of knowledge, namely, one which is committed to human emancipation. Habermas's model of human emancipation is one of what he calls 'unrestricted communication'. In such a situation communication is not susceptible to distortion through domination and violence. Each comprehends as an equal the utterances of another. Ricoeur's ambition is to derive a theory of ideology which captures the 'dialectic of the recollection of tradition and the anticipation of freedom'.[24] Ricoeur wants no more to dismiss the dialogues and discussion which have the authority of tradition than he does the controversies and debates which embody our aspirations for the future. Both spheres—one of the past, one of the future—suggest criteria whereby we can distinguish free and rational communication from misguided and erroneous reflection. From this point of view, it is essentially a social and ethical matter whether an utterance is or is not misleading.

Ricoeur rejects the orthodox Marxist-Leninist view of ideology because it conflates the notion of ideology as a world-view in general, with the critical notion of ideology as a misguided and confused account of experience. This is a difficulty we noted earlier. The ambiguity in Marx's account of ideology leads to two opposed views of the phenomenon, one positive and the other negative. Indeed, if one adheres to the latter—Marx's original critical—conception 'the paradox is that Marxism after Marx is the most extensive exemplification of its own conception of ideology'.[25] In the Soviet Union Marxism-Leninism appears to be nothing more than the ideology of the ruling class. In orthodox Marxism-Leninism the conception of ideology loses its critical edge. But Ricoeur is also not wholly happy with the original critical conception because it lends itself too easily to a separation of ideology and truth. Marx's own ideas are too readily portrayed as the truth and all else as ideology. Ricoeur is rightly sceptical of the possibility of any thinker achieving a sufficiently comprehensive standpoint to be able to look in this way—from outside—critically upon an ideology. For Ricoeur we must interpret an ideology from within that ideology. We have no neutral place from which to speak.

This is where Ricoeur draws upon the hermeneutic tradition. Ricoeur is attracted to the hermeneutic method because of the stress which it puts on the rootedness of our thinking in our society and history. As he puts it in his first proposition (aimed at developing a theory of ideology): 'All objectifying knowledge about our position, in a social class, in a cultural tradition and in history is preceded by a relation of *belonging* upon which we can never entirely reflect.'[26] All our thinking takes place with the aid of some fixed terms of reference. Many of these terms of reference we are not properly aware of, they may even operate unconsciously. Some are imposed by the necessarily finite nature of our knowledge. New information often comes at us from unexpected directions, and directions about which we are often ill-informed. To receive this knowledge in the first place requires a process of abstraction. We can only abstract on the basis of our already limited knowledge. Thus a 'coating' of ideology clings to all our knowledge.

None the less, we ought not to give up the goal of more rounded and complete forms of knowledge. Although always linked to an ideological frame of reference, we ought, in Ricoeur's view, to attempt as rational subjects always to distance ourselves from this frame of reference. As he puts it in his second thesis on ideology, 'distanciation, dialectically opposed to belonging, is the condition of the possibility of the critique of ideology'.[27] The first step in trying to comprehend the hold ideology has upon us is to stand back from our beliefs and preconceptions. In achieving this distanciation Ricoeur thinks it is possible to draw on a move familiar in hermeneutic philosophy. This move is to seek the level of 'pre-understanding' which corresponds with the level of actual understanding evinced in a text. The question to be posed of an ideology is: What constitutes the dialogue which lies behind the dialogue? In terms of Gadamer's philosophy this would require that we made evident the prejudices which give rise to the expression of views found in the ideology. Ricoeur does not see this process in the Marxist sense as one of unmasking hidden meanings but, rather, as a process of illumination and deepening of our knowledge, of interest both to the ideological thinker and the observer.

For Ricoeur the critique of ideology is, like ideology itself, tied to the here and now. This is why Habermas's interest-linked view of knowledge appeals to him. Just as the ideologists' utterances are tied to an interest, so Ricoeur thinks the critic must tie his views to an interest. This interest is in a different and better society. Such a new society will indeed have its own ideology, but presented as a future possibility, it may through its contrast with present thinking allow us to gain a more rounded picture of ideology now.

Thus, what the critique of ideology offers is not a whole new world fully free from distortion and misinterpreted forms of communications, but a different horizon from which to view what we now know. The theme of different horizons of knowledge in which the same phenomena appear in a less distant or more distant perspective is again drawn from hermeneutics. Hermeneutics offers a way of coping with this variety of perspectives which does not place one in an apparently superior position to all other perspectives. The hermeneutic approach recognizes the validity of various forms of historical understanding and sees the commitment to comprehension as one commitment amongst others. After all, ideologies are not constructed so that we can understand our society, they are constructed primarily with a view to living in it successfully.

It is difficult not to endorse Ricoeur's notion of a plurality of horizons of knowledge, especially when it is put in such a way that the effort to comprehend in a critical way is not abandoned. What leads to some doubts is Ricoeur's contention that we can never quite escape ideology. If this is so, how can we possibly be certain that what we hold to be an adequate explanation is not also ideology? There is an interpretative circle here from which Ricoeur never quite escapes. None the less, Ricoeur sums up his position powerfully when he says 'that the critique of ideology is a task which must always be begun, but which in principle can never be completed. Knowledge is always in the process of tearing itself away from ideology, but ideology always remains the grid, the code of interpretation.'[28] Thus we have a vision of social knowledge always hemmed in by the ideological dimension but never completely stifled by it.

NOTES

1. Ted Benton, *The Rise and Fall of Structural Marxism*, Macmillan, London, 1984.
2. S. Smith, *Reading Althusser*, Cornell, Ithaca, 1984, p.174.
3. Althusser, *Essays on Ideology*, Verso, London, 1984, p.6.
4. *ibid*. p.9.
5. *ibid*. p.20.
6. *ibid*. p.26.
7. *ibid*. p.32.
8. *ibid*. p.33.
9. *ibid*. p.36.
10. *ibid*. p.39.
11. *ibid*. pp.42-3.
12. *ibid*. p.44.
13. *ibid*. p.44.
14. D. Parfit, *Reasons and Persons*, Oxford University Press, 1985.
15. Althusser, *op. cit*. p.49.
16. P. Ricoeur, *Hermeneutics and the Human Sciences*, edited and translated by John B. Thompson, Cambridge University Press, 1984, p.223.
17. *ibid*. p.223.
18. *ibid*. p.225.
19. cf. H. Tudor, *Political Myth*, Macmillan, London, 1972, 65-70.
20. P. Ricoeur, *op. cit*. pp.226-7.
21. *ibid*. p.227.
22. *ibid*. p.232.
23. *Hermeneutics Reader*, ed. K. Mueller-Vollmer, Blackwell, Oxford, 1975, p.260.
24. P. Ricoeur, *op. cit*. p.100.
25. *ibid*. p.236.
26. *ibid*. p.243.
27. *ibid*. p.243.
28. *ibid*. p.245.

7 Conclusion

The purpose of this book has been to present and examine critically three theories of ideology; to look in depth at one particular ideology, the ideology of Fascism, and then to see what light the three theories shed on the particular ideology. I have concluded the study with a brief account of two more recent theories of ideology to demonstrate how the debate continues unabated.

What can be concluded about the three principal views of ideology we have examined from the critical discussion of Fascist ideology? The Marxian account provides probably the most powerful tool for placing in perspective an ideological tradition. By attempting to trace a political doctrine to what are regarded as its economic roots, the focus is valuably taken away from the realm of ideas to a sphere which undoubtedly has an important influence upon the growth and development of society. Fascism, for example, came to prominence in a period of great economic insecurity; it clearly appealed more to some social classes than others, and it was instrumental in developing economic forms along a novel and, for a while, successful path.

The Marxian view that Fascism grew from the threat posed to the middle and upper classes by the radicalization of the working class has, therfore, great plausibility. The modernization of the economies of Italy and Germany in the 1920s and 30s required greater labour discipline; but the paradox was that, as a result of the general political turmoil in Europe caused by the aftermath of the First World War and the Russian Revolution, the working class was becoming less and less disciplined and was demanding a greater share of the national income. The requirements of large-scale industry had to be met if the capitalist system was to survive. Fascist organization, discipline and terror provided the capitalist owners with the means to bring about the end of a more compliant and responsive labour force.

Doubtless, therefore, economic pressures helped lead to the success of Fascism. The Fascist could draw on a great reservoir of discontent amongst the peasantry and the lower middle classes concerning the prevailing direction of society. Rapid inflation, huge insolvencies, unemployment and cut-throat competition drove the small businessmen and artisans into the arms of the Fascists. The counter-radical appeal of Communism was not as attractive to these groups because of the possible loss of status it might involve. The egalitarian appeal of Communism did not, for the most part, match the lower-middle-class demands for security and prosperity. That Fascism did not offer a rational insight into the nature of society was an added advantage, since the economically-threatened preferred to forget and gloss over the causes of their discontents. Many were more prepared to face the imaginary foes of the Fascists rather than their true foes within society.

Thus, the strength of the Marxian view of ideology derives from its ability to relate political doctrines to their material context in the economic development of a society. The Marxist can at least *situate* an ideology within the society to which it belongs. Where the Marxian view breaks down, however, is in explaining the particular nature of an ideology. Much of European society in the 1920s and 30s required, from the Marxian standpoint, an authoritarian, anti-Communist and irrational doctrine to tide it over its economic problems. Yet the Marxian theory cannot explain why this doctrine took on the particular Fascist form.

Mannheim's account of ideology provides a far greater social psychological insight into the unique features of Fascism. Mannheim is more aware of how each individual has to draw on the collective consciousness in shaping his own thinking. The Marxian account, although tied to the fate of the working class, fails to recognize the almost ineluctable force the 'ideas of an epoch' exercise upon the individual. Caught in a cross-current of rapidly changing economic, social and political forces, neither individuals nor social classes can shape for themselves the ideas they adopt.

Mannheim's theory of ideology allows us to sense more clearly than the Marxian theory the manner in which human personalities are created by the institutions to which they belong. Although Mannheim brings up the optimistic notion of a 'free-floating intelligentsia' which may find itself in a position to influence the climate of the times, he is none the less a great deal more realistic about the circumscribed nature of the thinking of social groups. The intricacy and complexity of modern society will not allow social groups to develop autonomously their own political doctrines. For the most part, the individual members of these social groups are moved along by the ideas of the day. As their institutions crumble, so do their individual personalities. This insight is particularly appropriate in understanding the success of Fascism in the inter-war years. The lower middle class and the peasantry became vulnerable to the xenophobic, violent and extreme ideas of the Fascists as their businesses and farms crumbled around them. Fascism was a pathological response to what, for many, was a pathological situation.

Mannheim's theory is also more realistic about the manner in which the hold of an ideology can be broken. Essentially, Mannheim believes an ideology becomes dispensable only when it has outrun its social usefulness. This may appear to be stating no more than the obvious. However, what Mannheim maintains is that the full, negative nature of an ideology will not become apparent until its highest point of development and influence. At the time we cannot fully understand all the ideas and misconceptions which drive a society forward. Our involvement in society prevents the full transparency of such ideas. Mannheim appears correct in arguing that what he calls socially progressive ideas (i.e. Utopias) are not fully distinguishable from socially backward ideas (i.e. ideologies) until we are properly able to look at a period from a historical perspective.

From Mannheim we gain a clear sense of the unavoidable nature of ideological frameworks of thought. Even when we are attempting to escape the influence of an ideological tradition we remain, as Ricoeur also stresses, hemmed in by its limits. Even the Marxian revolutionary perspective has to acknowledge the limits set by the pro-capitalist ideologies it opposes. Where Mannheim's theory most falls down is, as we have seen, in its view of the role that the socially conscious intelligentsia can play in mitigating the effects of an ideology. Mannheim believes that intellectuals, although they cannot be fully free from ideological perspectives can, nevertheless, render themselves relatively free. As a consequence, Mannheim paints too sanguine a picture of what intellectuals can achieve by way of giving their societies a new, planned, direction. He does not deal with the objections that might be made to his Utopia of democratic planning and he does not foresee the fierce opposition that those claiming intellectual superiority might face from established upper social groups and those rising in the social order. Just as some politicians and members of the public have a prejudice in favour of academic thinking, there are those who, perhaps regrettably, have a deep-seated prejudice against academic thought and the ivory tower with which it is associated. What price the 'free-floating intelligentsia' of Mannheim against Mussolini's *squadristi* and Hitler's stormtroopers?

The great strength of the Oakeshottian view of ideology is that it takes into account more readily than Marx and Mannheim the nature of everyday practical thinking. The average individual is as much concerned with what use a number of ideas might have as with their truth. This is brought out in Oakeshott's view of practice as a distinct world of ideas. From the Oakeshottian standpoint, we are wholly mistaken in thinking we can apply scientific, historical or philosophical ideas to our practice. Indeed, Oakeshottians see this as one of the cardinal errors of ideological thinking. The ideologist, according to the Oakeshottian, falsely seeks to apply concepts which have their true function in other worlds of ideas, such as history and science, to the world of practice.

This trait we can see clearly in Fascist ideology. Hitler enthusiastically took the Darwinian notion of the 'survival of the fittest', and applied it to society with disastrous consequences. Another feature of ideological thinking which the

Oakeshottian theory brings to light is the political ideologist's lack of respect for established canons of rationality. This is well exemplified in the Fascist tradition. As Manning stresses, for the political ideologist what counts are those ideas which bring to you the most supporters and followers. The Fascists had no respect for academic criteria of truth; rather, they took up those ideas and trends which would maximize their support. Thus, the thorough inconsistency of some ideologies, particularly Fascist ideology, can be explained. It matters little if one fact or one theory contradicts another in the Fascist ideologist's account of the world; provided the account animates individuals into sharing the ideology and joining the movement, it serves its purpose fully.

Ideologies are directed towards practical ends. Ideologists either wish to change the world in certain ways or to prevent it from being changed. The canvassing and recruiting Fascist party member is anxious to gain adherents for his or her cause. The confrontation with others is not where the ability to debate rationally is of primary importance; rather, what is required is the means and the ability to assert and counter-assert in a dogmatic fashion. What the Fascist ideologist requires is not the truth, but rather a set of easily assimilated ideas which add up to a well-founded prejudice. As Ricoeur notes, for an ideology to succeed, the intellectual level at which the argument is pitched has to be reduced from that of high theory and scientific verity. This non-scholastic feature of ideological thinking is overlooked by both Marx and Mannheim. They ignore the fact that, for the majority of individuals, getting on and doing well in the world are far more important than thinking clearly and acting morally. For the ordinary person, thought and ideas are a means to an end rather than ends in themselves. The ordinary person is prepared to tolerate logical and moral inconsistency in a way which Marx and Mannheim fail to recognize.

All theorists of ideology would agree that an ideology represents a practical attitude to the world. The Oakeshottian argues that this practical attitude to the world can be nurtured in a context in which traditional notions of coherence and truth need not play a prominent part. The world of practice produces its own unique criteria of adequacy. Oakeshottians would therefore dispense with a critical notion of ideology on the grounds that all practical thinking is coloured by ideology. The important choice the individual has to make is not between ideology and truth, but between rival ideologies. The ideology one chooses to adhere to is not dictated by scientific, historical or philosophical considerations but one's personal preferences and tastes.

This is, I believe, too facile a view. Although human practice will not yield in the same way as the enquiries of science and history to the criteria of truth, truth and consistency can none the less play a role in our social and political life. To dispense with the negative concept of ideology is ultimately to dispense with the use of the term altogether. If all practical thinking is ideological, then ideology becomes indistinguishable from practical thought. The concept makes sense best as a critical conception of social thought. Just as the Oakeshottian will admit there are grounds for distinguishing science from practical thought, there are also good grounds, advanced by Marx and Mannheim, for distinguishing ideological social thought from coherent and consistent political and social theory. Those grounds cannot be discovered solely in the theory of ideology since they derive ultimately from social and political theory. The critique of ideology forms, therefore, an essential introduction to the study of social and political theory.

From our study of three concepts of ideology we can, therefore, conclude that none of the three theories is, in every respect, superior to the others. Rather, each adds a new dimension to our understanding of ideology. Each theory can be improved and be made more sophisticated by taking into account the strengths of another. We see this in the contributions of Althusser and Ricoeur. Althusser's theory of ideology is essentially a modification of the Marxian view, and Ricoeur's theory draws explicitly from Mannheim's theory. In this process of improvement and sophistication, Marx's account can be regarded as forming the base which is nowhere wholly refuted; Mannheim suggests some sensible modifications to this foundation; and the Oakeshottian view adds a measure of practical realism not present in the first two theories. As we see from Althusser's and Ricoeur's contributions, the process of building up a comprehensive theory of ideology is never complete. There are always further blocks to be added to the building. What cannot be denied is that the three rival theories provide a valuable edifice.

The Problem of Ideology
I am finally going to look at a very difficult question. What makes the problem of ideology such a contentious one for modern social studies is the unavoidable way in which it raises the issue of the relation of action or practice to knowledge. Theorists of ideology realize that the two are inextricably intertwined. Marx and Mannheim are immediately conscious that the question 'What is true?' cannot be answered separately from the question 'What ought we to do?', and even the Oakeshottians concede that in the practical sphere each seeks a 'true' vision of reality.

The realization that the question of truth and the nature of right action are inextricably interlinked is not a new one. In ancient Greece Plato and Aristotle drew together the theory of knowledge, ethics and politics in their philosophy. Plato's theory of forms provided him not only with an account of the formation of our knowledge but also with a conception of the good that shapes his political thought. With him the just state is brought about through the knowledge of philosophers. Aristotle is not so sanguine about the role of philosophers, but even with him, Plato's greatest critic, it is to philosophy we look for the guide to sound action. The rule of seeking to pursue the 'golden mean' in all our actions derives from Aristotle's cautious, analytical view of knowledge.

During the Middle Ages Thomas Aquinas was also a notable representative of the view that human practice and knowledge are inextricably intertwined. His catholic vision of the world derives from a conviction that what we know to be true must guide our action. Divine law, natural law and human law are all linked by the grace of God and the perceptiveness of human knowledge. The same vision is to be found in the work of the great seventeenth century Dutch philosopher, Spinoza. For Spinoza there is but one reality, which he calls Substance. Through our reason we become acquainted with this Substance which indicates to us not only what is the case but also how we should act. In knowing God or Substance we know also how to behave ethically.

The trend which decisively separated knowing and acting in modern times was the trend towards adopting in all spheres of knowledge the methods of natural science. Many philosophers such as Hobbes, Gassendi, and Hume came to the conclusion that such was the advance in our understanding of the natural world—brought about by the development of sciences such as astronomy, physics and chemistry—that success in all other fields could be guaranteed if only we adopted the same experimental methods. Thus the practice of natural science came to dominate in many individuals' minds the proper pursuit of knowledge. It was not surprising that other forms of human practice appeared less adequate mediums through which to realize and employ our knowledge. In comparison with the quantifiable and experimentally proven knowledge of the successful natural scientist, the knowledge of those employed in other human pursuits such as the law, ethics, religion, literature and politics appeared second rate.

This is the position today and this is what makes the problem of ideology such a difficult one. Most people still concede only one model of 'true' knowledge, namely the knowledge of the natural scientist; so the pretensions of those involved in human practice to be dealing with problems of truth can simply be discarded. But we can rapidly see that all forms of human action and thought do not fall into the sphere of natural science. Science deals only with a small, quantifiable, regular and predictable aspect of our experience. As human individuals we have to exist in other realms, such as that of nation, society, home, school and immediate locality. In these realms we can naturally want to know 'What is the case' as much as we want to know 'What ought we to do?'. Within the realm of the predictable and quantifiable, natural science may be able to help, but there is always a residue of questions of value where knowing and acting necessarily overlap.

As we have seen, the Marxian theory of ideology tries to overcome this difficulty by acknowledging the link between action and theory and suggesting there is one clear form of (revolutionary) action that leads not only to the truth but is also ethically correct. This Marxian view is a restatement of Plato's radical position, but in a different form. Instead of the philosophers on their own having the key to right action, Marx thinks it is the proletariat moved by the most advanced theories of philosophy that has the key. In changing the world, according to Marx, you prove the correctness of your theories and the incorrectness of contemporary ideologies. In medieval England, for instance, it was difficult to prove to the society at large that the established doctrine of the divine right of kings was a mistaken one. However, as medieval structures began to crumble it was, as John Locke found with his *Two Treatises of Government*, a far easier task to show the king's right to rule was not derived from God or Adam. English society in the late seventeenth century was simply more receptive to the truth than the previous tradition-bound feudal society. But it would be wrong to suggest that Marx has the whole truth. That we are, under different circumstances, more receptive to the truth does not mean that changed circumstance will confirm any fondly-held theory. Looking to the future provides no certain guarantee of the truth of today's contention. Should circumstances alter in an unanticipated way this may lead to an apparently cogent theory being proved entirely wrong, just as an apparently entirely inadequate theory may be proved correct by a similarly unanticipated turn of events. Thus, in itself, future practice provides no sure guarantee of the truth of a theory, it merely provides a context in which a theory can be shown to be true. As Marx himself is aware, to show the correctness of his critical views on capitalist society he has also to draw on more formal criteria of truth derived from the sciences and logic.

Mannheim also was not prepared to dispense with the usual canons of logical argument in presenting his theory of ideology. He seems equally to value highly the effort to maintain coherence and to be true to the facts in presenting his ideas. Like Marx, though, he allows a role for future society in deciding the overall cogency of social ideas. His distinction between ideology and Utopia rests not on formal criteria of truth but upon whether or not a set of social ideas turns out to be socially progressive. There are fewer clues with Mannheim, however, as to what we might expect to be socially progressive ideas. Mannheim is content for the decision to be made after the fact. He expresses the hope that the most advanced intellectuals in a society may have an intimation as to what will turn out to hamper progress and what will accelerate it, but these intellectuals are given no guide as to how they might fulfil their task.

Have we to imply from this that the only possible conception of knowledge we can hold is a relativist or relationist—as Mannheim calls it—one? Is knowledge, as with beauty, always in the eye of the beholder or, more correctly, with Mannheim, in the eye of the free-floating intellectual? Ricoeur with his concept of ever-widening horizons of knowledge grasps the nettle of relativism without quite getting the better of it. Ricoeur fails to provide clear criteria with which we can distinguish between one or the other horizon. He implies they are all equally valid. His notion that we are ever entrapped in ideology but always (as limited human creatures) seeking to escape it, conveys the problem posed by the study of ideology but does not adequately answer it. Ricoeur offers no guide as to how we might judge the degree to which we have escaped the net of ideology.

I have no comprehensive answer to the problem. However, I suggest that an adequate answer might have to run along these lines. Truth, I would argue, cannot be separated from activity which is life-enhancing to the human species. Contrariwise, it is human life-enhancing activity which reveals the truth. This is the hall-mark of the sphere where we have appeared to enjoy the most marked success in attaining knowledge, namely natural science. What is revealed to the natural scientist by his researches increases the possibility of extending our control over nature. Even if our scientific researches do not lead to an immediate extension of our control over nature they may, none the less, help us to avoid pit-falls laid before us by nature. The study of the theory of ideology is valuable on similar grounds. Through the greater knowledge of the thinking of individuals and the nature of social beliefs we attain, we may be put in a position where we are able to improve our social environment. The desire to know what underlies our thought and actions is not, according to this view, a neutral desire. We want to know, the better to live. Knowledge and a healthy existence are intimately interlinked. No one would, on the one hand, dispute that the more know-ledgeable is a doctor the greater is his or her ability to cure. Yet, on the other hand, great scepticism would nowadays be expressed about the assertion that the more knowledgeable are individuals about their ideas and society the more they can contribute to their well-being and the well-being of society. But it is precisely this contention that makes best sense of the theory of ideology. By knowing more about the origins and limitations of our social and political thinking, we can live fuller and more valuable lives.

Underlying a viable theory of ideology is a vision of the good life. The student of ideology cannot stand empty-handed in the face of the visions of the good life incorporated in the ideologies under consideration. Taking advantage of the theories of ideology already to hand, each must build up a view of social thought which is beneficial both to himself and the community. Guidance as to what is life-enhancing can be gained by a critical examination of ideologies themselves, but an even sharper view can be gained from the study of social and political theory as a whole. There is an unavoidable circle of knowledge here which is constructive rather than destruc-tive: to know what constitutes ideological thinking we must know what a healthy vision of society consists in, but to know what such a healthy vision is we must be able to reject what is misleading or ideological. This circle can never be fully broken, it is simply one which we must enter through the critical study of the theory of ideology.

Select Bibliography

Abercrombie, N. et al., *The Dominant Ideology Thesis*, Allen & Unwin, London, 1980.

Althusser, L., *Essays on Ideology*, Verso, London, 1984.

Althusser, L., *Lenin and Philosophy*, New Left Books, London, 1971.

Arendt, H., *The Origins of Totalitarianism*, Harcourt, Brace, Jovanovich, New York, 1973.

Barth, H., *Truth and Ideology*, University of California Press, Los Angeles, 1976.

Bell, D., *The End of Ideology*, Free Press, Glencoe, New York, 1960.

Benewick, R. T.; Berki, R. N.; & Parekh, B. (eds), *Knowledge and Belief in Politics*, Allen & Unwin, London, 1974.

Benton, T., *The Rise and Fall of Structural Marxism*, Macmillan, London, 1984.

Blackburn, R. (ed.), *Ideology in Social Science*, Fontana, London, 1972.

Carlsnaes, W., *The Concept of Ideology and Political Analysis*, Greenwood, Westport, Connecticut, 1981.

Drucker, H., *The Political Uses of Ideology*, Macmillan, London, 1974.

Durkheim, E., *The Division of Labour in Society*, Free Press, New York, 1974.

Elster, J., *Making Sense of Marx*, Cambridge University Press, 1985.

Engels, F., *Anti-Duhring*, Lawrence & Wishart, London, 1969.

Feuer, L., *Ideology and the Ideologists*, Blackwell, Oxford, 1975.

Gadamer, H. G., *Truth and Method*, Seabury Press, New York, 1975.
Gouldner, A., *Dialectic of Ideology and Technology*, Macmillan, London, 1976.
Gregor, A. J., *The Ideology of Fascism*, Collier-Macmillan, London, 1969.
Gramsci, A., *Selections from the Prison Notebooks*, Lawrence & Wishart, London, 1971.

Habermas, J., *Knowledge and Human Interests*, Heinemann, London, 1972.
Habermas, J., *Theory and Practice*, Heinemann, London, 1974.
Harris, H. S., *The Social Philosophy of Giovanni Gentile*, University of Illinois Press, Urbana, 1966.
Hegel, G. W. F., *Phenomenology of Spirit*, tr. A. Miller, Oxford University Press, 1979.
Hegel, G. W. F., *Philosophy of Right*, tr. T. M. Knox, Oxford University Press, 1971.
Hirst, P., *On Law and Ideology*, Macmillan, London, 1979.
Hitler, A., *Mein Kampf*, Hurst & Blackett, London, 1939.
Horkheimer, M., & Adorno, T., *Dialectic of the Enlightenment*, Allen Lane, London, 1973.

Jakubowski, F., *Ideology and Superstructure in Historical Materialism*, Allison & Busby, London, 1976.

Kettler, D.; Meja, V.; Stehr, N, *Karl Mannheim*, Ellis Horwood, London, 1984.

Laquer, W. (ed.), *Fascism*, Penguin, Harmondsworth, 1979.
Larrain, J., *The Concept of Ideology*, Hutchinson, London, 1979.
Larrain, J., *Marxism and Ideology*, Macmillan, London, 1983.
Lenin, V. I., *What is to be done?*, Panther, Oxford University Press, 1970.
Lenin, V. I., *Philosophical Notebooks, Collected Works*, 38, Foreign Languages Press, Moscow, 1960.
Lichtheim, G., *The Concept of Ideology and Other Essays*, New York, Random House, 1967.
Loader, C., *The Intellectual Development of Karl Mannheim*, Cambridge University Press, 1985.
Lukacs, G., *History and Class Consciousness*, Merlin Press, London, 1971.

Mannheim, K., *Ideology and Utopia*, Routledge & Kegan Paul, London, 1976.
Manning, D. (ed.), *The Form of Ideology*, Allen & Unwin, London, 1980.
Manning, D., *Liberalism*, Dent, London, 1976.
Marx, K., *Capital*, Vol. 1, Lawrence & Wishart, London, 1970.
Marx, K., *A Contribution to the Critique of Political Economy*, Lawrence & Wishart, London, 1971.
Marx, K., *Writings of the Young Marx on Philosophy and Society*, edited and translated by L. D. Easton and K. H. Guddat, Anchor Books, Doubleday & Co., New York, 1967.
McLellan, D., *Ideology*, Open University Press, Milton Keynes, 1986.
Mueller-Vollmer, K., *Hermeneutics Reader*, Basil Blackwell, Oxford, 1986.

Nolte, E., *Three Faces of Fascism*, Weidenfeld & Nicholson, London, 1965; Mentor, New American Library, New York, 1969.

Oakeshott, M., *Experience and its Modes*, Cambridge University Press, 1933.
Oakeshott, M., *Rationalism in Politics*, Methuen, London, 1967.
O'Sullivan, N., *Fascism*, Dent, London, 1983.

Parekh, B., *Marx's Theory of Ideology*, Croom Helm, London, 1982.
Parry, G., *Political Elites*, Allen & Unwin, London, 1970.
Plamenatz, J., *Ideology*, Macmillan, London, 1971.
Popper, K., *The Open Society and its Enemies*, Routledge & Kegan Paul, London, 1977.

Remmling, G. W., *The Sociology of Karl Mannheim*, Routledge & Kegan Paul, London, 1975.
Ricoeur, P., *Hermeneutics and the Human Sciences*, Cambridge University Press, 1984.

Seliger, M., *Ideology and Politics*, Allen & Unwin, London, 1976.
Seliger, M., *The Marxist Conception of Ideology*, Cambridge University Press, 1971.
Simmonds, A., *Karl Mannheim's Sociology of Knowledge*, Clarendon Press, Oxford, 1979.

Talmon, J. L., *The Origins of Totalitarian Democracy*, Secker & Warburg, London, 1952.

Therborn, G., *The Ideology of Power and the Power of Ideology*, Verso, London, 1980.
Thompson, J. B., *Critical Hermeneutics: A Study in the Thought of Paul Ricoeur*, Cambridge University Press, 1981.
Thompson, J. B., *Studies in the Theory of Ideology*, Polity Press, Cambridge, 1985.

Vajda, M., *Fascism as a Mass Movement*, Allison & Busby, London, 1976.

Williams, R., *Keywords*, Fontana, London, 1980.
Woolf, S. J., *The Nature of Fascism*, Weidenfeld & Nicholson, London, 1968.

Index

133